# HOW TO ENJOY A FAMILY FIGHT

*Will Cunningham*

QUESTAR PUBLISHERS, INC.

PHOENIX

HOW TO ENJOY A FAMILY FIGHT
© 1988 by Will Cunningham
Published by Questar Publishers, Inc.


Printed in the United States of America


ISBN 0-945564-04-X


*Cover design by Bruce DeRoos*

TO MY LOVING WIFE, CINDY

*When the labor was long,*
*You were my epidural*

# CONTENTS

## Part III: STYLES

## Part IV: THE MASTER OF CONFLICT

# Introduction

JUST THE OTHER DAY I saw a classic conflict outside my office window. The church where I work as a counselor has an elementary school, and that particular day was Field Day—filled, as tradition would have it, with fun games like the three-legged race, the gunnysack race, the egg toss, and more. The afternoon finale was the ultimate in gender-clash: boys versus girls tug-o-war.

I watched as the two sexes squared off for battle. The girls giggled nervously. They had little to lose, it seemed. The boys, on the other hand, clenched their teeth, chewed their tongues, and made a huge show of digging their hightop tennis shoes into the ground for added leverage. They had life at stake.

The whistle blew, the rope stiffened, the boys turned crimson, the girls giggled...then panic broke out on the boys' end. The girls were inching them closer and closer to defeat.

Tempers rose. Accusations flew. "Pull harder, Todd!" "I am! Why don't you?" "I am!" But nothing helped. Suddenly, with a heave, the gigglers sent the boys sprawling.

Shrill, unison voices called out in that sing-song pattern we all learn early in life: "You boys are weaklings! You boys are weaklings!"

Up jumped the boys from the ground, quickly engaging themselves in all sorts of manly behaviors such as shoving each other, pretending to be fascinated with a nearby soccer ball, or staring off with hands on hips and that faraway look men get when they've been beaten badly but don't want to discuss it. I had to laugh.

To the male reader I say, *Let's not kid ourselves.* As men, you and I both know we would behave in much the same way (maybe worse) if the women at the office challenged the men to a duel of some sort, and won. Interview my wife, Cindy, and she'll tell you: When I perceive I've lost a conflict with her, I go about life as if nothing in the world existed below the five-foot-two mark (which happens to be her height).

We'd all rather win a fight than lose one. When was the last time you set out to lose a fight with your spouse—or anyone else? Probably never.

As I watched the triumphant gigglers and the smitten warriors make their way back to the classroom, I was reminded of the many couples I see in counseling each week. Marital tug-o-war takes place often in my office, and many a time the session ends with a self-righteous winner and a bedraggled loser walking out the door. However, I make one thing very clear to them, and you'll want to grasp it too:

> *If you set out to win a marital or family conflict, in the long run you will always lose.*

By definition, if there is a winner in a fight there must also be a loser. And a marriage or a family is no place for losers. If the losers lose often enough, they'll either harden themselves and resolve to win (at a tragic cost) the next time, or they will quit the game altogether. The wife who is continually proven wrong by her uncompromising husband will lie awake at night planning ways to snare him. The teenager who feels his parents never listen to him will eventually quit trying to communicate. "Yeah, yeah, you're always right," he says when another conflict arises—and then walks off, intending fully to do the very deed his parents adamantly oppose.

So remember: If you're a person who must win...do it on the playing field or on the court, but please resolve now *not* to do it in a conflict at home.

I've seen enough couples and family members trying to defeat each other that I finally decided to write a book that teaches them how to fight right. I hope it will help you take the edge off your conflicts, making them constructive experiences rather than downers.

This book is for anyone—single or married—who is weary of fighting destructively with the people he or she loves. It's for the multitude of those with battered egos and bruised memories of painful relationship conflicts. It's for the individuals with abusive tongues and uncontrollable anger. It is for the iron-fisted parent and the rebellious teen. It's for the husband who knows deep down there must be a better way to respond to conflict with his wife than making a safe getaway in the family car.

Wherever two or more people have a continuing relationship, there will eventually be conflict. Are you married? There will be conflict. Are you single and living at home with your parents? There will be conflict. Are you the parent of a single son or daughter living at home? There will be conflict. Do you have a roommate? There will be conflict. Is dating a part of your life? There will be conflict. Do you share a job environment with co-workers? There will be conflict. Conflict is everywhere!

And whenever there is conflict, there can be one of only two outcomes: We will either hurt—even destroy—each other; or we will build up each other and benefit from the experience. It all depends on whether we fight wrong or fight right.

Fighting wrong comes naturally, but rarely are we given instruction in how to fight right. Consequently, we experience the worst results from our conflicts rather than the best.

To turn that situation around at your house, read on...and discover perspectives and principles that could change forever the way you and your family fight.

# part i

# A Gift to Be Opened

# 1

# The Gift of Pain

BEE CREEK BRIDGE was an unlikely place to begin a romance. And I hadn't planned to stop there.

It was a cold, sleepy December morning, but I was feeling warm all over. This was a chance of a lifetime. I had waited so long for this, and now I deserved it.

Courting Cindy had not been easy. She was different. She was a challenge. Perhaps that's why I persevered as long as I did. Now she was coming around...beginning to see things my way.

As we drove down southern Missouri's Highway 65, I was surrounded by late autumn witnesses to my falling in love with precious Cindy—the Canadian geese landing in Ford Field, the mist rising from the dark water of Taneycomo, the smoke of burning oak and ash curling from cabin chimneys and resting in Ozark hollows.

We were driving north to Springfield to watch a group of high school boys from Branson play basketball. Both Cindy and I had spent almost the last half-year in Branson in a ministry to kids. It had taken me months to convince Cindy we could be more than just ministry partners. Tonight, after the game, we were going on our first official date. Little did we know we were in for a much longer date than we had planned.

The bridge stretched over the valley like a hand over a yawn. A hundred and fifty feet below was its namesake, wandering homeward to cold-black Taneycomo. A mist climbed up from the creek, rising until it transformed the iron trestle into a covered bridge. We drove onto it.

Out of the fog came two headlights, approaching fast...and in the wrong lane.

Cindy never saw them. She was looking down at her lap, reading a card I had made for her. I saw the truck, but didn't have time to swerve. The two vehicles smashed face to face, the sound of metal on metal waking the morning. Our Honda Accord bounced, spun, careened into the bridge guardrail and bounced off, and halted.

Then silence.

Semiconscious, I began a feeble attempt to assess injury. I felt like a marionette with its strings cut, limp and lifeless. I tasted blood. I heard a crunch as I tried to move. Broken glass. Broken teeth? No, they were all there. I felt my lips—split clean through, top and bottom, and numb. My mind registered the sight of a bent steering wheel, a missing windshield, a tape deck, a glove box, a hand brake. Hand! Cindy? Cindy!

I saw the torn card...her ripped jeans, red and wet...white bone, jagged. Her limbs were twisted around the wrecked engine that protruded, hot and hissing, into her lap. She turned and moaned; her shattered hands clawed the air, beckoning for help. I heard sirens...men running.

I shivered.

Then...darkness.

Christmas morning. After weeks of morphine, traction, splints, casts, surgery, stitches, hospital food, and armies of well-meaning visitors, Cindy and I finally were allowed to see each other. The nurses wheeled our beds into the sunroom at the end of the hall and left us side by side, alone. Dawn, like an angel, came softly through the panes at the foot of our beds, and out over the valley we saw the highway meandering across the frozen, hardwood floor of the Ozarks. Had we harbored bitterness about the accident, that winding stretch of asphalt might have seemed like a thin black snake, coiled and ready to strike. But we saw only a road, eclipsed by the beauty of the infant snow spread around it like a white dust ruffle.

"My hands don't look so good, do they?" Cindy said, breaking the silence.

She was right. Her hands were covered with thick purplish scar tissue from the lacerations she received when the windshield exploded in on us. She was also still sporting a raccoon eye.

"I'll always hold your hand, Little C," I answered. "You've just never given me a chance."

We both burst out laughing—I belly-laughed so hard that my hip, now secured with screws, felt on fire. But if this was courtship, I thought, give me more pain. Cindy reached across the space between our beds, and for the first time grasped my hand.

"I love you, Will Cunningham."

"I love you, too, Cindy."

A single, silver tear appeared in the corner of Cindy's blue eyes, and she spoke again.

"I really love you, Will."

We laughed and cried some more that Christmas morning until nurses wheeled us back to our rooms. It was the beginning of real healing for our bodies, and the birth of true love for each other—a lifetime of love.

I share this story with you simply because it reflects a basic premise of this book:

*There is gain in pain.*

My high school football coach used to say that too. I can still hear his voice during hot August two-a-days: "Cunningham! Quit your griping and get back down in your stance. No pain, no gain! Do you hear me, Cunningham? No pain, no gain!"

I didn't believe it then, and perhaps you don't believe it now. It flies in the face of the evidence, doesn't it? Our bodies ache, our minds are in turmoil, our marriages and families are struggling. How could there ever be enough good in all that to justify the pain we're going through? And yet, though we seldom rise above our own suffering long enough to see it, it's true: There is gain.

Looking back at my life since December 5, 1981, I see two things: pain and gain. There was the pain of loss. I lost the feeling in my entire left side as a result of the crash. Even now as I type, I'm often forced to watch the keys because I cannot feel them beneath my left hand. I also lost my ability to play the guitar and to participate in some of my favorite sports—things I have since re-learned, but only after a long road back.

If I could relive the past and escape that pain, yet it meant having to miss out on even a fraction of the good that came from the wreck—especially a beautiful marriage with the girl of my dreams and a handsome new son to boot—then I would not cash in a single twinge. There is gain in pain!

## The Thrill of the Fight

Conflict is painful, especially in our marriages and families. But there is gain even in your relationship conflicts—real, actual benefits. A fight can be a delight.

As a counselor, I meet daily with couples experiencing conflict. At their first appointment, many come in like two rabid pit bulls. With these, as with any couple I counsel, one of my key goals in the early stages is to instill hope. Even the tiniest speck of hope is better than none at all.

So to couples in obvious conflict I'll start by saying, "I am so thrilled the two of you are fighting," and then watch their expressions. Jowls snap shut. Flaring veins recede. The angry stare is replaced by a peaceful look. Some of them eye me as if I were either sadistic or a lunatic.

But I continue: "It's the people sitting silently at opposite ends of the couch who I worry about. At least the two of you are presenting a lot of material we can work with here." Often the couple's angry stares are replaced by a look of peace. In this more relaxed setting, we can now get down to the business of channeling all that destructive fighting into constructive, profitable conflict.

But why is it so difficult to see gain in pain? After all, many things we desire require us first to go through pain. The peace of mind from maintaining adequate financial records requires the monthly pain of balancing a checkbook. Keeping or regaining good health may mean taking distasteful medicine or even submitting to a surgeon's blade.

In our relationships, however, most of us consistently avoid the pain of conflict. Consequently our anger and frustration mount so high that sooner or later, like the checkbook that has gone unbalanced for several months, we begin to see red.

I don't believe we are born with a disdain for personal confrontation. We are taught it. We learn early that a perceived or real opponent is someone to be either avoided or crushed—and we seldom have all it takes to do the latter.

By the time we're adults with families of our own, we've learned not to rock the boat. Instead, when the troubled seas of conflict loom on the horizon, we either abandon ship, or angrily and carelessly sink it ourselves.

*For every "I do" in our land today . . .*
*there's an "I don't love you anymore";*

*for every family vacation . . .*
*a family separation;*

*for every matrimony . . .*
*an alimony;*

*for every wedding announcement . . .*
*a marriage annulment;*

*for every "Little House on the Prairie" . . .*
*a foreclosure due to divorce.*

And for every family breakup, there are who knows how many situations in which family members are merely enduring, rather than enjoying, one another. In nearly all these cases, wrong responses to conflict are to blame.

✳ ✳ ✳

*Twenty years old. Tears brimming.*
*Tight brows. Tongues spewing.*

"I'll tell you exactly where you can go," she yells as he turns to walk out. "You can go straight to—"
"Go there yourself!" he interrupts, not looking back.

*Door slam. Deep sob. Dying marriage. Day begins.*

✳ ✳ ✳

*Fifty years married. Fighting silently.*
*Futile endurance. Frozen frowns.*

"She's been making us late to church for as long as

we've been married," he reminds himself again, "and I'm sick and tired of it."

Looking in the mirror to make one last adjusting tug of her sweater, she sees the reflection of his rigid form in the doorway. "Why he has to always pick Sunday to put on his grouchiest face I'll never know," she tells herself. "I'm ashamed to be seen with him."

*Sanctuary door. Singing choir. Same pew. Sullen silence.*

\* \* \*

*Jams and skateboards. Gels and mousse.*
*Jam-box rappin'. Generation gap.*

"You will not go out looking like that again! Every time you step out the door, you are an embarrassment to your father and me!"

"Yeah, right! Like you guys aren't an embarrassment to me every time my friends come over! You're the problem, not me!"

*Bedroom retreat. Bored with life.*
*Bad grade spiral. Borderline rebel.*

\* \* \*

## Rattler! Rattler!

Seven years ago in southern Missouri I was camping with a few friends on an island in the middle of Table Rock Lake. In our charge was a squirmy bunch of about twenty boys. We were having the time of our lives, doing whatever we wanted without a thing to fret over for three days. If we chose to have chocolate pudding

with pancakes for breakfast, then so it was, and the same
for sailing, water-skiing, sun-tanning, or swimming.
Someone had pushed the time button, and life away
from the island was on hold.

Early one morning, our tranquility was interrupted by
a loud chorus of boyish screams, which aren't much different from girlish screams. The adults who were awake hur-
ried in the direction of the noise, and quickly met a
stampede of wide-eyed urchins. "It's a rattler! It's a rattler!" one of them shouted as the herd thundered past us.

Below us on the beach the rest of the boys danced like
tribal warriors, jabbing sticks toward something at their
naked ankles. Stopping to pick up a rock or two in case
we needed a weapon, we quickened our pace to the
beach. By now the rather large snake had been killed,
but not before biting one of the daring braves on the leg.
Rolling on the ground, he screamed in pain, "I'm gonna
die! I'm gonna die!"

Luckily for him, the "rattlesnake" turned out to be a
harmless, aged water snake. The only immediate threat
the boy faced was from an extra-large dose of teasing
from the other boys.

Relaxing around the campfire at the end of the day,
we all had a good laugh at ourselves—that is, all except
the boy who had originally identified the "rattler." He
kept insisting that "rattlers back home really do look like
that." We howled into the night.

If you typically view a looming family fight as a "rattler," you will undoubtedly respond as these boys
did—by either running away from the confrontation, or
defending yourself with cruel methods. By viewing conflict negatively, you have sadly limited yourself to only
those two approaches: fight or flight.

Neither works well in marriage. Let me tell you
about two couples who would agree.

## Anton and Daria

With a string of obscenities and a slam of my office door, Anton made his exit. His wife, Daria, stared at the sofa pillow next to her. She had begun to cry. Her bruised left cheekbone was momentarily covered by the veil of warm tears. I extended to her a box of tissues, a small consolation.

This was our first meeting together. After a long silence, Daria began.

"It's not usually like this. The hitting, that is."

"What is it usually like, then?" I asked.

"Well, just words I guess."

"Words like the ones he was using when he just left?"

"Yes."

"Do you use those same kinds of words?"

"Yes."

I continued: "What do you want to do about this?"

"What else can we do?"

When our hour was over, Daria dabbed her eyes, being extra careful with the bruised one. After she left, five words whispered over and over in my mind. What else can we do? What else can we do? What else can we do? What else...?

There is not much else we can do. Rattlesnakes always call for retaliation or retreat. Scared to death of the viper they saw in their relationship, Anton and Daria chose retaliation. With words and fists, they struck.

## Don and Meagan

Other couples choose to retreat.

Both Don and Meagan came from homes where conflict was handled by withdrawal rather than warfare. By the time I saw them for premarital counseling, each had

been married three times. Their six previous marriages
had died early deaths, all victims of extramarital affairs.

Products of rigid, legalistic upbringing, neither Don
nor Meagan had ever seen their parents engage in a rela-
tional conflict. In both families, fighting was not the
"Christian" thing to do. When Don's parents were upset
with each other they often didn't communicate for days.
Incredibly, from the time Don was thirteen his parents
neither ate together nor slept in the same room. Every
family conflict that arose was swept under the rug. Not
surprisingly, both of Don's parents suffered from depression—a common indicator of anger turned inward.

Meagan's background was similar. Her parents, too,
refused to speak with one another when a problem came
up between them. But Meagan's troubles were com-
pounded: Her father, whom she termed "sternly religious," often directed against Meagan the anger he had
toward his wife. Meagan's high school years were characterized by extreme hatred and resentment for both her
parents.

She married early, her wedding resembling a jail-
break more than a joyous union. Much like her parents'
household, the sound of conflict was seldom heard in her
new home. Instead of dealing with normal negative
emotions that arose between them, Meagan and her first
husband crammed those feelings deep inside themselves,
adding fuel to an inner furnace of anger. For two years
they endured their silent struggles with each other. Then
Meagan sought solace in another man's embrace, which
led to the dissolution of her first marriage. Her second
and third marriages were virtual replays, except that this
time her husbands were the unfaithful partners.

In Don's similar story of three marriages, three affairs,
and three divorces, he and his wife in each case fought by
default, always withdrawing and shutting each other out.

## *Take Another Look*

Which approach do you think is worse—the destructive conflict Anton and Daria experienced, or the silent, gnawing trap of avoided conflict that victimized Don and Meagan?

Is your family following one of those patterns—either blasting away at one another, or silently lifting the rug and whisking away your problems? If so, I challenge you to take another look at what you're reacting against. You'll probably discover that your "rattler" is a harmless creature after all. In fact, it's a source of benefit—of gain.

In my own family, conflict does at times seem particularly dangerous. Quite often my emotional panic button flashes at the first sign of a fight, and in my head throbs the message: "Rattlesnake! Rattlesnake!" At that point I try to focus my mind on this important statement:

> *Whenever a conflict in my family starts to resemble a "rattlesnake," I will immediately try to view it instead as a gift to be opened.*

Conflict is really a gift—the gift of pain—from which you and I can benefit by receiving and opening, even though it hurts. Anton, Daria, Don, and Meagan all wish they had.

Picture for a moment a beautiful church sanctuary where an elaborate wedding is in progress. Follow me to the front of the church and let's listen as a handsome groom and his glowing bride ascend the altar steps to state their vows.

Turning to face his beloved, the young man begins. The hush over the sanctuary deepens, as the congregation strains to hear his every word—

"...to be my wedded wife, and I do promise and covenant, before God and these witnesses, to be thy loving and faithful husband, in plenty and in want, in joy and in

*the gift of pain*

sorrow, in sickness and in health, as long as we both shall live."

Pause.

Friends and family wipe their eyes, awaiting now the young woman's words in return. But to everyone's surprise, the groom continues:

"And furthermore, I do promise and vow to fight toe to toe with you, my lovely wife, each and every day for the remainder of our years together."

The church rafters ring with the sudden gasps of enraged relatives, while the stunned bride turns ashen.

What a nightmare! But consider for a moment the countless newlyweds who walk arm-in-arm from churches everywhere without a clue of the disaster awaiting them—the disaster that befalls every husband and wife who refuse to open the gift of pain. This groom with the unexpected vow had the right idea by including an important but so often overlooked commitment: to face conflict head-on instead of running from it or lashing out angrily. There at the altar he was affirming his wise willingness to receive and share with his future spouse one of the greatest of all wedding gifts...the gift of pain.

As I sit in our living room I'm surrounded by wedding gifts to Cindy and me: the coffee table with its bruised shins; the desk with the drawer that needs fixing; and on top of the television, one of the five thousand or so brass candlesticks we received. Besides being wedding gifts, they have something else in common: In varying degrees they are tarnished, gouged, chipped, scraped, and torn—they are all wearing out. It makes one wonder: Does anything nowadays really last?

The answer, of course, is *Yes*—right relationships last, when we nourish them with care. And you can do your part to make your marriage a lasting one by making this promise as a precious gift to each member of your family: "I will view our conflicts as positive, and I will do everything I can to mutually resolve them with you."

As you consider that commitment, look squarely at the conflicts in your life. Force yourself to visualize them: The argument you had last night with your wife, or the disgust you feel each time your junior-high son walks by wearing that earring, or the quarrels that accompany every trip to the in-laws. What do you see in these conflicts? Is a rattlesnake glaring back at you? If so, close your eyes tightly, count to three, and take another look: There in front of you is a magnificently wrapped box. On the gift tag are bold red letters: *The Gift of Pain*.

Let your natural curiosity take over now, as you carefully open the box to see what's inside....

# part ii

# Rules

# 2

# The Governor and Mr. Bibtucker

UNTIL I WAS FIFTEEN or so, athletics for me was like walking a dog with no legs—a real drag! I was the original Norman Rockwell character, long and lean (with emphasis on lean). I could have passed for the skinny kid at the beach on the back of Marvel Comics. But when my latitude finally caught up with my longitude, I began enjoying the competitive side of me that had been dormant during my early years, buried under mounds of kicked sand. Today, I enjoy a good game of anything as much as the next person.

So what do athletics have to do with the way your family fights?

Every family fight is like a game in sports—for example, you have two opposing sides, both wanting to win, and the contest usually takes place on the weekend. But one element from the world of sports is probably missing in your conflicts at home: You're playing without rules, so the players are left wide open to injury.

I believe a lack of knowledge causes most people to fight without rules at home. Their "coaches" simply never taught them the rules. The results are nasty—as in Jessica's case. When I met Jessica she was a grown woman in her late twenties who criticized others (and herself) constantly. She entered every disagreement with chin down and dukes up. She was the queen of verbal artillery (though a lonely queen indeed), and she rarely lost a battle.

But Jessica was a victim, not a victor. Her childhood had been spent in a house filled with bitter strife without any rules—a house where, in her words, "sitting down to dinner was like going to war...except you never knew who your enemy was." Assault was part of the daily dialogue, malignant messages that Jessica heard so often she easily memorized them: *Don't you know when to quit eating? I swear, Jessy, you are so fat.*

When she left home, such words still spun in her head—and echoed in her speech to others. The game with no rules had claimed another casualty.

Whatever happened to the guidelines for a good, clean fight? In our generation, at least, I believe they've gotten lost in the funhouse of personal rights—the me-first clamor. But once there was a time when the game of conflict was less brutal and every player emerged a winner...

As you unwrap the box marked *The Gift of Pain*, flinging aside the wrapping paper and reaching within, you will discover another small box inside. It's labeled *Rules* in silver letters, and inside is an account of the very first game—the granddaddy of all games—and the story of how its rules were invented.

## The Big Game

New Woods Ferry was a town of contrasts. Next to the skeletal architecture that lined Main Street, the beauty of persimmon and dogwood trees looked fake and propped-up.

This was only a reminder of a once teeming town, the residue of happier days before the falling out—before the people fled to Adam's Crossing. Now only animals remained.

A visitor walking down Main would hardly notice the Rug Emporium or Morton's Tannery or Saul's Saloon. These were not much for noticing. Only two things stood out: the silence, and the great, white house at the end of the street.

There were rumors about that house. Some said the Governor still lived there, but certainly not like before. He used to address the town once a week from the lofty balcony. Below it on the front lawn, huge parties often were thrown while he looked on, and the whole town was invited. There was dancing and singing and story-telling long past bedtime...and children stayed up for it all.

And food...my was there food! Roast pheasant and hot beef pies. Piping cider in mugs as big as watering cans. Large baked potatoes, cracked open and drizzled with butter. Corn and cornbread and candied yams and seven or eight kinds of salad. There were cakes and pies and tarts and streudels...all moist and sweet and steaming. And every gentleman washed his own dishes.

There had never been a fight, as we know it, in New Woods Ferry. Once at Saul's Saloon, a man lost his savings in a card game. He didn't swear or stamp around or try to hit someone. He merely thanked his friends and walked out the door. The next day the whole town pitched in and made it all up to him.

But a time came when the people of New Woods Ferry wanted a change. They suddenly began grumbling about "orders from the balcony." Some men stirred up the entire town to a frenzy, until they all arose one night and fled miles away to a corner of the Governor's domain called Adam's Crossing. But here their desire for better things went unmet. The happiness of their time in New Woods was left behind, traded away for an unsatisfying independence. A fairy tale told by the fire...this was all that remained for them of the old days.

In New Woods Ferry the streets were empty and the town was silent. The animals spent their time hunting for food or lying around in the shade of the boardwalks along Main. A few of them—they were nicknamed "the Dreamers" by the rest—sat faithfully on the Governor's lawn, hoping they might catch a glimpse of him or hear his voice calling from above.

## Footsteps on the Balcony

One morning, just a glimmer past sunrise, the Dreamers heard a noise. The sound was unmistakable...footsteps on the balcony! As the animals looked up, the sunlight climbing over the railing made the form of the Governor clearly discernible. He was still in his pajamas.

"Top of the morning, my friends!" exclaimed the Governor, smiling down at his menagerie. "All is well?"

"Oh, yes, your Lordship!" crowed the rooster. "Everything is perfect. We are exceedingly happy." This, of course, was not at all true, because the animals had been exceedingly *un*happy for quite some time.

"I concur," snorted the pig, between mouthfuls of breakfast. "The food here in your town is like none I have ever tasted."

The Governor smiled. "Please continue," he said.

"The climate really is very nice," the fat tabby announced, scratching her back on a fence post.

"Just the right amount of sunshine," yawned the groundhog, as he crawled lazily out of a nearby hole.

(These too were a lie, because even the weather had been beastly since the townsfolk left.)

From underneath a patch of lush, soft clover, came a tiny but adamant voice. At first it was unnoticed by the gathering of animals, who chatted on. But its repetition soon became an annoyance, first for the canines with their keen sense of hearing, then for others. Finally the entire band of creatures stopped to listen, each leaning expectantly toward the spot of undergrowth. The wee voice spoke again:

"Your Highness, and Most Governly of Governors, with all due respect, I do have one small complaint."

"Alright," the Governor replied, "but to register a complaint you must first at least show yourself."

The animals waited.

With a rustle of clover and a shuffle of assorted hooves and paws to make room for the newcomer, out stepped a smart, little beetle.

He was dashing in the sunshine, all winsome and brave as he walked forth. He wore a red vest with a gold watch tucked into the right breast pocket, the chain of which hung nearly to his knees. He tipped his top hat lightly as he advanced into the circle of onlookers. And though he had legs aplenty, he carried a shiny, black cane.

Glancing around, he spotted an acorn and with some assistance from a squirrel he wrestled it to the center of the lawn. There, to ensure that he was heard, he climbed atop his little stool, stood on tiptoe, turned his face up toward the balcony, and cupped his hands to his mouth for good measure as he began to shout.

"Your Most Majestic of Majesties, sir, I regret to comment on this, but as I have mused and perused the situation here in this most lovely of towns, I have noticed that we, the citizens of it, are lacking one small thing."

"Do proceed," said the Governor.

"Most Benevolent of Benefactors...well, sir...you see...uh...oh dear." It seemed the daring spokesman was losing pluck.

"Speak up, please, my little friend," chuckled the Governor.

The beetle took a deep breath, then blurted out, "We have no *games*, sir!"

The air promptly filled with laughter from the balcony. It began like the sound of summer cicadas crooning from the dark canopy of a maple forest, then burst into bellows. It was enough to send birds on the wing and the smaller ground creatures scampering under the safety of the boardwalks. From there they peered out, trying to make sense of this new phenomenon. After all, there had been no laughter in New Woods Ferry for what seemed like ages.

The voice from the balcony continued. "Games? Of course you want games! But I've already given them to you."

Animals all over town were awake by now. Puzzled by the commotion at the big white house, they had gathered to observe.

"The games are all there within you," continued the Governor. "The *will to play* is what you need. You must make your own games. I give you my permission. Go! Be free! Run! Jump! Frolic! Frisk! On with it, my little ones!"

With that, the town was transformed into a carnival of celebration. They were going to have games! Dogs and cats chased madly up and down Main Street. Pigs rooted. Calves skipped. Birds matched each other note for note from the highest limbs in New Woods. I have no doubt that the cacophony of joy was heard as far away as Adam's Crossing.

## The Granddaddy of Games

The animals went right to work inventing the very first game. The beetle, whose name was Mr. Bibtucker, was a natural leader and took charge immediately.

"First, we must have a ball," he stated enthusiastically. "What good is a game without a ball?"

The animals looked confused. "What's a ball?" one of the dogs said. (Dogs will often speak up that way, for they are unashamed of their ignorance and have very little concern for social standing, as evidenced by the fact that they regularly eat from trash cans and think nothing of it.)

Mr. Bibtucker scratched his head, annoyed by the dog's question.

"Well how am I to know? Am I supposed to know everything?" said the beetle. "Besides, I can't be bothered with that right now. Why don't you and your dog friends invent one?"

So they did. (This explains why today most dogs like to play ball—they're really quite proud of their invention.)

With that matter out of the way, Mr. Bibtucker went on to delegate other tasks. "Uniforms! Hoops! Goal posts! Whistles! Look alive," he commanded. "There's no time to waste. Baskets! Ball caps! Skis! Skates! Checkers!" The diminutive dictator was obviously enjoying his position of management, and he gave every creature a part, which they eagerly carried out. Only the pig, whose assistance the dogs had requested in designing the football, turned down an assignment. He opted to help invent the concession stand.

At last came the day for the big game to be tested.

On the outskirts of town the assembly of animals stood in a grassy field waiting for instructions from their leader. Mr. Bibtucker had spent hours mapping plays and developing an elaborate play book. On paper it really was a glorious game...much more so than any game you or I will ever dream of playing. (It would not be proper for me to try explaining the game here because I could never do it justice. But I will tell you that it was meant to be played on ten different fields with twenty-five kinds of balls, and each player was to change uniforms at least five times.)

Something, however, was missing from the plans... yet Mr. Bibtucker couldn't quite tell what it was, so onward the project went.

After singing the New Woods Ferry anthem (an idea the birds came up with), everyone turned towards Mr. Bibtucker. The little beetle was perspiring heavily. What with all the rushing around, checking uniforms, inflating various balls, and all the other things that go along with being in top management, he had forgotten that it was his job to start the game. Mr. Bibtucker hesitated for a moment (like the pause when you've done all the packing for a long vacation and are about to walk out the door, but suspect you've left something.) With a puzzled look still on his face, he then pressed a whistle to his lips and blew.

What happened next is hard to tell and still sound believable, but I will try. Clamor, chaos, pandemonium! Feathers flew and fur bristled. Hooves and hindquarters flashed in a mad scramble. A dog went sailing by in the air. Thud! Uniforms were getting ripped and grass-stained. Flags were waving. Whistles were blowing. Mr. Bibtucker was running...waving...screaming.

"Enough! Enough! Stop playing! Stop the game! Stop it all this instant!"

It took at least thirty minutes of shouting and jumping up and down before anyone even took notice of Mr. Bibtucker, and another thirty minutes for the crowd to obey him. Finally, there was order.

Mr. Bibtucker looked out across the field. Goalposts were toppled. Every ball was flat and lifeless. Bits of fur and uniform were scattered here and there. His game was a failure. And he had used every single one of his ideas. There was nothing more he could do but sit down, right there on the field, and have a good cry. So he did.

Then a wise old owl, who had been watching from a nearby tree, flew down and landed next to the weeping Mr. Bibtucker. The owl, Hornrim by name, knew enough to keep his distance (for it is never smart to approach a beetle in mourning), and so from a few feet away he asked, "To whoooom do I have the misfortune of listening as he pours out his woes and contritions?" (This is exactly what you expect from a wise old owl, who is, of course, too learned to say, "Who are you?" and "Why are you crying?")

"My name is Bib…(sniff)…tucker. And I'm crying because I'm a failure. Now go away."

"Oh," said Hornrim. "Poor, pitiful Bibtucker. I would offer you my condolences, but as sure as death and taxes you wouldn't want them."

Mr. Bibtucker stared at the ground, but Hornrim knew he was listening. The owl continued, "It is lamentable, though, when such a strong-witted somebody as yourself ceases to set his wits to work."

Mr. Bibtucker was puzzled.

"I think what he means is that you shouldn't give up," offered the tabby, who with the other animals had drawn in closer to their wounded leader.

"Yes, exactly. That *is* what I'm trying to say," said Hornrim. "But what you need are rules, my friend.

Rules are of a necessity.  And whoooooooooooo among us is sagacious enough wherewith you might inquire about these rules?"  At this point, Hornrim ruffled his feathers a bit and pretended to be deep in thought on this question, while being sure all the while that he himself was the obvious answer.

"The Governor!" shouted Mr. Bibtucker, getting to his feet.  "We'll go to the Governor!"

The animals let out a grand hoorah and rushed off with him, leaving Hornrim muttering something about the inability of lower animals to recognize a known academician if he flew up and shouted at them.

## The Governor's Decree

When everyone arrived at the great white house, it was evening.  There was a bit of nip in the night air, the kind that reminds you of the tail end of a drink of cider. On the balcony was the Governor, wearing a mackinaw and leaning heavily on the railing.  Smoke rolled from his meerschaum pipe. He was deep in thought.

"Hullo, sir!" called Mr. Bibtucker.

"Well, hullo back to you!" said the Governor.  "I was thinking of you just now…I hope the game is going marvelously.  It is faring well, is it not?"  (Of course, he knew all along that it was not.)

"Well…no, not exactly," said Mr. Bibtucker.  "We're having a bit of trouble with keeping order.  The owl says what we need are rules.  You wouldn't happen to know much about rules, would you, sir?"

The Governor chuckled.  "Rules?  Do I know about rules?  Of course I know about rules.  I know something about everything…and everything about anything.  And I can help you, if help is what you're asking."

"Yes!  Yes!" cried Mr. Bibtucker.  "Please help us!"

The Governor invited them in from the cold and he fed the fire with oak and cedar kindling. Then he opened his cupboard and took down all manner of lovely eatables which he spread out before the hearth for himself and his little friends. Outside, the autumn wind blew loudly. But inside the Governor's den, every soul was warm as crumpets. After eating, the Governor lit his pipe and leaned back in his corner chair, losing himself in a cloak of ringlets and shadows. Only a glint of chin and eyebrows showed as he launched into an explanation of the rules.

He spoke of intricate rules that carried great importance, and trivial rules that mattered only once in a great while. He told of silly rules and serious rules and he even said a word or two about rules for making up more rules. As he came to each one, he wrote it down in ink, turning the parchment from side to side in order to catch the firelight. The animals went on nibbling and tippling...getting more excited each minute by the Governor's words. When the last rule was spoken, and the game was resurrected, Mr. Bibtucker did a somersault or two across the room where he came to a halt at the Governor's feet. Looking up, he said, "And what, sir, should we call our game?"

The Governor thought for a moment, then rose from the dark corner and strode to the mantel. After a last pensive puff, he raised his pipe toward the ceiling and said, in a low and serious tone, "Citizens of New Woods Ferry: By the power in me, I decree that the game forever more be called...'Fight!' "

And so it was.

## *"Fight"*

With its new rules, the game of "Fight" was every bit as glorious as Mr. Bibtucker intended it to be. Everyone enjoyed it...even Hornrim, who seemed less stuffy the more he played. A good "Fight" became the answer to a host of problems in New Woods. For example, minor disputes such as which mudhole belonged to which pig, or which dog was privy to which bone, were often settled by a lengthy round of the new game. Usually the whole town could not resist getting involved each time a new match began.

"Fighting" soon became a daily part of the animals' lives and they eventually forgot there had ever been a time when it didn't exist in their town. Winters would come, bringing an intermission as many of the animals hibernated, and those that didn't were busy scratching around in the snow for food. But in the spring the game was always revived once more, and New Woods Ferry came to life again.

## Farewell to New Woods

One day, as the animals were preparing for their first fight of the new season, a man and woman emerged from the woods that bordered New Woods Ferry on the north. Most of the animals had never seen a human being other than the Governor, and if their sudden wonder was not enough to keep them from offering a greeting, the looks on the strangers' faces were. Both travelers seemed burdened by a bitter sadness.

As the two drew closer, a few of the elder animals began to recognize them. The old, gray hedgehog turned and whispered to the fox, "By the Governor's best pipe, I do believe these are the former mansion groundskeepers!"

"But that can't be," the fox replied in a hushed tone. "They were always such a happy pair. These two look as if they've been sentenced to serve some awful penance."

The two sad figures looked as if they intended to

walk on by the animals without a word, which they might have done were it not for Mr. Bibtucker.

"Pardon me, Your Gloominess," said the beetle, bravely breaking the silence. "I and my friends here couldn't help noticing your dismal countenances. Do tell us, is something the matter?"

The man began: "Yes, much is the matter. You see, my wife and I have been banished by the Governor from this lovely country."

Suddenly the assembly of animals was abuzz with questions and statements and disputes.

"Banished by the Governor?"

"What?"

"Did you hear...?"

"Banished by the Governor?"

"Banished?"

"He said...?"

"Banished!"

"But the Governor would never..."

"*Quiet!*" shouted Mr. Bibtucker. "Let's hear them out!"

The man continued: "It's true! We were causing no harm on his land. We tilled the ground, pruned the plants, watered his crops. But now look at us... banished to a distant country. I ask you, is that the way a loving benefactor should act?"

Before the animals could answer, the woman began to speak: "But don't you think we should tell them, dear? It was really was our fault. We—"

"We?" the man interrupted, close to shouting. "*We?* If I recall correctly it was you and your friends who talked us into the rebellion. So keep quiet with all this talk about *WE!*"

He turned again to the animals. "The fact is, we got into an awful fight with the Governor."

"A 'fight'? Well that shouldn't be a problem for you,"

said Mr. Bibtucker. "We fight with each other every day and we're all the better for it. In fact, the Governor himself gave us rules and taught us how to fight."

"Well and good," said the traveler, "but the Governor is a crafty one. He'll trick a fellow into believing all is right as rain, and then pull the stopper. Look at us. He once gave us something, too. It was called, 'free will,' and he made us believe we were the lucky ones for receiving it. Then we found it wasn't 'free' at all. No indeed. There's an awful price to be paid for having it."

"Tell us more," said Mr. Bibtucker. By now the animals had formed a circle around the two travelers and were listening intently.

"That's right. You'd be wise to listen. You soar like eagles now, but it won't be long before these wonderful rules of yours will clip your wings and you'll come crashing down. *And the Governor will watch you fall.*"

"What are we to do?" inquired Mr. Bibtucker, persuaded now by the man's testimony.

"You must rid yourselves of these rules and of the Governor's grasp on you. And purge yourselves of this game you call Fight, before you find out what it's really like to be in a fight with the Governor. Do it now! There's not a moment to lose."

Frightened, the animals buried the parchment with the rules written on it, then left to follow the man and woman. As they passed by the last buildings at the west end of Main, Mr. Bibtucker paused and gazed down the street. He had hoped to see the Governor one last time...but the balcony was empty.

## Long Live the Rules

Somewhere, somehow, someone must have dug up that old parchment, because rules have popped up all over the world in all sorts of games. And each game benefits enormously from them. I am sad to say though, that Fight, the granddaddy of all games, has not turned up anywhere...at least not in its original form. Oh yes, we still fight with each other every day but, as I said before, we do it without any rules. We scream, kick, curse, cry, run away, and run each other down. I guess I should say we fight like the animals did before the Governor came to their aid.

Maybe your family fights are so out of hand that you, like Mr. Bibtucker, feel the best you can do sometimes is sit down and cry. But I have good news for you. The same rules that the Governor gave to the animals that autumn night by the fireside are available to you today. You can read about them in the daily sports page or watch them from the couch on a lazy Sunday afternoon of television. They are the rules that make up every sporting event known to mankind. Please pay strict attention to the following chapters, because they are the meat of this book. These chapters contain the rules that could help you and your family recapture the lost game of "Fight."

Long live the rules!

# 3

# Offsides

Pick the right time to fight.

"WHAT DOES 'OFFSIDES' mean to you?" I asked this question to a premarital class at Cherry Hills Community Church, and most of the answers had something to do with timing. Timing is crucial in the game of football. All a player has to do to wreck a potentially great play is to make one poorly timed move before the ball has been snapped. Offsides is a rule that is frequently violated on the gridiron and even more frequently in our daily conflicts. Just like the lineman who jumps across the line of scrimmage prematurely, when we jump the gun in a conflict we ruin the possibility of resolving that conflict very soon.

## Fred and Terri

Fred and Terri had been married long enough to have experienced the rigors of raising a family. With two small children and a third on the way, they rarely had time for each other. Terri was feeling as if she was at the bottom of the totem-pole of importance in Fred's life. His job, his hobbies, his TV time—all seemed to come before her and the family. Terri had begun to think, *If this is married life, then I'd better prepare myself for a life of misery.* They had been fighting for quite some time before they ever sought counseling.

Early in our counseling sessions I asked them, "When do most of your fights occur?"

"In the evening, about dinner time," they both agreed.

A penalty flag immediately flashed in my mind: Offsides! I asked each of them to describe a typical day for them. Terri described a day full of household chores and errands, kids to entertain and potty-train, armloads of laundry, bills to pay, a ringing phone to answer—and all magnified by the nauseating effects of early pregnancy. Fred spoke of lost accounts, broken business deals, endless meetings, and unrealistic deadlines.

"What is the last thing that you want to do at the end of a day like that?" I asked. Smiles broke out across their faces. Both had understood my point. They were violating the Offsides rule by fighting at the wrong time.

Soon they realized they could handle conflicts more successfully if they chose a better time to conflict. As they talked about their grievances in my office, they immediately noticed how much easier it was to discuss them away from the normal end-of-the-day weariness and havoc.

They discovered that Terri needed time and attention from her husband in the evening to rejuvenate her love for him and to restore her sanity after a long day with the kids. Her pattern, however, had been to virtually assault Fred at the door with demands for his time, which offended Fred. What he most needed was a little time to unwind, to exercise, and to free his mind from the stress of the day. As these needs had clashed, their tempers rose, (while the kids screamed louder and louder in the background). Fred and Terri were penalizing their entire family by jumping Offsides in their fighting.

They agreed that Fred would first have his brief "relax time" after he came home, while later in the evening he would spend time with Terri, or take care of the children so she could relax. They also agreed to refrain from bringing up disagreements in the early evening before they had relaxed. They had learned this lesson:

> *There is a right time and a wrong time for most fights. Seek to delay conflict when you are stressed out physically and emotionally. Mutually decide upon a later time to resolve the conflict.*

Ask yourself these questions:

> *When is a poor time for me to conflict with my loved ones?*
> *When am I at my best?*
> *When am I at my worst?*

Maybe your spouse is not a morning person but is more communicative in the evening. If so, don't try to resolve problems in the morning.

## Teaching Children about Offsides

You can easily teach your young children about the offsides rule. Help them to take "time outs" when they are angry with you, with a sibling, or with a playmate.

Even a child of three or four is not too young to learn this concept.

When your child is extremely angry (which may be often, since his little will is just beginning to bump up against the wills of other people), help him see that his anger is "too big" at the moment and that when it becomes "smaller," it can be talked about.

Set an egg timer for ten to fifteen minutes. Involve your youngster in some activity such as a craft or coloring. Better still, do that activity with your child. When the timer goes off, sit down with your child (or with the two offended parties) and talk about what is bothering each person. Help your child see that controlled anger is acceptable, but that sometimes it is best to wait before talking, so that the anger has a chance to get "smaller."

# 4

# Delay of Game

*Learn to listen.*

IMAGINE YOU'RE a football quarterback. Your team is huddled on your opponent's five-yard line, five seconds remain in the game, and you hope to score a touchdown to win the game. But you have a problem: None of your teammates is listening to you as you try to call the winning play. Your center is busy trying to convince the other players that *his* play will work best. The left tackle is talking about a referee's bad call back in the first quarter. The rest of the team is grumbling that you don't know what you're talking about in the first place.

Suddenly a whistle blows. Your team is being penalized for Delay of Game—too much time in the huddle. The ball is set back five yards, and on the next play you fail to score. The game is over, and you walk from the field a loser, feeling separated from your teammates and wondering why you even bother to play.

The same thing happens in marriage and family conflicts when we're guilty of Delay of Game because of failing to listen to each other. Unfortunately, the stakes at home are much higher and the consequences more lasting than on the football field.

Most of us are poor listeners by nature. Especially in

a conflict, we're like tadpoles with alligator mouths —we do much more talking than we should.  Think about your own tendencies when you're experiencing conflict with someone.  Do you *hear* the words the other person is saying?  Do you carefully consider the meaning and the feeling behind the words?  Or do you tune out the other person and anticipate what you will say when your opponent's lips stop moving?  I admit that my tendency is to build my own case in my mind while the other person is talking, and then to jump into the argument the second I have the opportunity.

## *Tom and Linda*

I witness a lot of verbal ping-pong between angry couples in my office.  Back and forth the volleys fly, each person winding up for a harder smash the next time.  Tom and Linda were much like this.

"You are so picky about the way I keep house," Linda shouted.

"Oh, really?" Tom shouted back.  "I guess I just don't happen to care for lint all over everything the way you do."

"The fact is," Linda replied with steadily increasing volume, "You don't care for much of anything—including me!"

Tom and Linda had been like this during each of our three counseling sessions.  I had heard enough.

"Hold it!" I said.  "Is this the way you two normally fight at home?"

Tom laughed.  "Are you kidding?  This is mild in comparison."

When Tom and Linda first came for counseling they said they loved each other, but just couldn't understand why they fought so much.  Fighting was a habit they couldn't seem to stop. The fact that they fought, I now sensed, was not the problem. The problem was the *way* they fought. For starters, neither of them listened to the other. Even when they weren't fighting, they constantly interrupted each other.

I asked Tom and Linda to try a listening exercise that was new to them. As they practiced it over the next few weeks, it frequently prevented their disagreements from escalating into full-scale battles.

I call this exercise "Check It Out," and it has often helped Cindy and me to avoid Delay of Game.

### CHECK IT OUT

- Person A says what he or she is feeling.

- Person B says, "What I hear you saying is _____" (repeating as much as can be remembered of Person A's message). Person B then asks, "Have I heard all that you are trying to say?"

- Person A can answer:
    - "Yes"; or,
    - "No, here is what I am trying to say…"; or,
    - "Yes, you heard part of my message, but here is the part you missed."

Repeat this process until Person B has heard and understood Person A. Then reverse the procedure, with Person B being the message sender and Person A the message receiver.

Once both of you have heard and understood the other person's feelings or opinions on a particular matter, ask each other: "How do you want me to change?" or, "What can I do to make the situation better?"

Repeat the Check It Out process again, with both parties listening to and repeating what the other person says.

This may sound to you like something that could happen only in Bob Newhart's office, and never in real life. Here's a story, though, that may convince you of its practical usefulness.

## *Dinner at the Doubletree*

Early in our marriage Cindy and I recognized my tendency to get defensive and to counterattack with my own airtight case when I'm in conflict with her. I vowed to work hard at changing it. But every now and then I slip back into my old habits.

When I began writing this book we were in the last few weeks of Cindy's first pregnancy. We realized that soon we would no longer be a couple, but a trio. Life would never be the same. So I planned a special date for the two of us, a sort of final fling before we took on the responsibilities of child raising. I secretly made reservations at a posh Denver hotel, and Cindy was completely surprised when the day came and I told her my surprise. We changed into nice clothes and arrived at the hotel that Friday evening to enjoy a wonderful candlelight dinner. Everything was perfect...except that I had forgotten to bring enough money.

The problems associated with this kind of oversight are obvious, but you really need to know more about Cindy and me to understand why I was in particularly hot water. I am a "big picture" man. Cindy goes for details. I love to plan creative, grandiose events and vaca-

tions and dates. Cindy is more concerned with the little
things like, "Do we have enough money for this?" or,
"Can we make it from here to there on this amount of
gas?" or "Do you *really* think it's appropriate for you to
wear jeans to this dinner party?" I've often dropped the
ball in the details department, but on this particular date
I thought I had been doing rather well in this area for
some time.

We were just finishing dessert when the waiter
brought the check. I glanced at the total and gulped! I
knew the amount in my wallet was at least twenty dollars
short. Matters got worse when I had to leave the table and
go up to our hotel room to get money from Cindy's purse.
By the time I returned, Cindy wasn't interested in making
conversation. *Oh, great,* I thought, my defenses rising.
*Here I plan this terrific weekend getaway and Cindy focuses on
one minor mistake* (at least I thought it was minor). In silence we rode the elevator back up to our room.

When we got inside, I sat quietly in a chair in the corner, hands clasped tightly behind my head, eyes focused
only on things above the five-foot-two mark. Cindy sat
down in the chair next to me and began a conversation.
I, however, was determined not to listen or talk. Suddenly, I thought to myself, *Wait a minute. I am violating the
very rules I share with people in my office every day. I have a
choice to turn this fight around right now or I can delay the
game by not listening to Cindy—and ruin the entire weekend
by my stubbornness.*

As much as I didn't want to, I began to hear Cindy's
words and to phrase them back to her as clearly as I
could. Cindy's voice softened, her body visibly relaxed, I
moved a bit closer to her, and soon we were holding
hands and talking rather than shutting out each other.

As I let her words sink in, I realized how embarrassing it was for Cindy when people perceived her husband

as scatter-brained. Cindy wasn't attacking me—she wanted to be proud of me, and my failure to pay attention to details made it difficult for her to do that. Every time I failed to use my head, I was hurting Cindy. All this became clear as I let her words strike home.

Within minutes our conflict was resolved. Cindy complimented me for my romantic efforts in planning the date and I apologized for my lack of detailed planning. We were spared a costly penalty for Delay of Game. The next day, as I settled our exorbitant hotel bill, I recognized just how much more our conflict could have deepened, and how costly the penalty might have been. Instead, we left the hotel refreshed and feeling like winners because we followed a simple rule:

> *Actively listening to one another in a conflict always moves people closer to resolution. Failure to actively listen "delays the game."*

Here's a version of "Check It Out" especially for children, to help them get the hang of positive conflict resolution. I call it "Pass the Ball."

### PASS THE BALL

Needed for playing the game:

1. One football (or any substitute object small enough to be held by a child)
2. Two or more children who are at each other's throats

Let's suppose little Billy has a beef with younger brother Johnny. Billy comes to you with a quivering lower lip and says Johnny just bit him. Loud wails can be heard from the other end of the house. You rush down the hallway into Johnny's bedroom, where you see him sniveling with his face buried in a pillow. He looks up, spies Billy at your side, and points an accusing finger: "He bit me first!" he says with a dramatic sob.

By now you sense the role you're being asked to take in this episode, and the idea of playing both judge and jury this afternoon does not excite you. Wouldn't it be heaven if Billy and Johnny could resolve their own conflicts? After all, you have enough conflicts of your own.

Though it's unrealistic to expect Billy and Johnny to resolve their conflicts alone, they *can* do it with your help. You can escape the judge-and-jury role by trying this "Pass the Ball" exercise:

1. Ask Billy and Johnny to sit down face to face. (You'll have to referee this exercise.)
2. Hand Johnny the ball. Ask him to tell Billy why he is upset. While he collects his thoughts, tell Billy to keep quiet as long as Johnny has the ball.
3. When Johnny is finished talking, hand the ball to Billy and have him rephrase what Johnny said. Then have Billy tell his side of it, with Johnny doing the listening and rephrasing.

In this version of "Check it Out" the "ball" is just an object of security for the youngster who is stating his case. He knows that as long as he holds it he will be heard. Of course, this exercise will not free you totally from being an administrator of justice, but at least the process will be characterized by less whining and screaming.  Most importantly, with this game you can teach your children the valuable lesson that *conflicts CAN be talked out*.  They don't have to be shouted out.

You need not wait for a conflict to benefit from this exercise.  As a family, begin "passing the ball" at the dinner table when everybody seems to be talking at once.  Whoever holds "the ball"—the saltshaker, a candlestick, a serving spoon—has the floor.  Families that truly learn to listen to one another will never have a problem with Delay of Game.

One of my favorite short poems is this one by Shel Silverstein:

> I have found the secret of friendship.
> There's really nothing to it.
> I simply tell you what to do,
> And you do it.

Sounds fairly simple, doesn't it?  Think of all the needless misunderstandings that could be avoided if only one person in a relationship did the talking.  The problem, of course, is that everyone wants to be the talker, not the listener.  Silverstein's verse accents humorously the one-sided communication we selfishly desire, but must get beyond if we want to avoid Delay of Game in our relationships.

Psychologists have noted that when people sense they're being listened to, that simple fact alone goes far in motivating them to solve many of their problems.  People love to know they're being heard.  But active listening by itself is never enough.  The "Check It Out" process does little good if we do nothing more than hear one another's words.  We must take it one step further:

> *We must actually learn
> each other's language.*

## Becoming Bilingual

Let's return to our final huddle in the football game. Same scene. Ball on the five-yard line. Five seconds to go. Your team is behind by three points with a chance to score the winning touchdown. The crowd is screaming.

Suddenly, the coach sends in a new quarterback from the sidelines. The brawny bunch of men look up from their circle to see the second-stringer trotting towards them. "Oh no!" they mutter. "Not *him.*"

As the young rookie arrives at the huddle, ducks down on one knee amid the massive linemen, and begins giving his teammates instructions, we understand their frustration. «*Á droite, mes amis,*» he says. «*Peu de chose, n'est ce pas?*» He speaks only French.

"Peu de chose, n'est ce pas?" mimic his teammates dutifully, with no idea what they are saying. They break the huddle and line up in formation.

«*Gardez la foi,*» he adds in closing. "Gardez la foi," they repeat. They break the huddle and line up in formation.

The Frenchman hovers over center. «*Un, deux, trois, hut-hut.*» The ball is snapped and—you guessed it: Disaster! Because no one understood the quarterback's instructions, each man just did what he thought best. There was no touchdown. No victory. No celebration. The players walked from the field depressed and disgusted.

Do you speak your teammates' language or do you just mimic their words? Author and marriage counselor Norm Wright often tells couples in premarital counseling: "Turn toward each other and take a long look at the person you are about to marry. Do you realize the person looking back at you is a foreigner? You come from different cultures, and you observe different customs.

How will you ever be able to communicate unless you both commit right now to learning each other's language?" Dr. Wright is right. Each of us must do everything possible to understand the meaning behind the words our family speaks.

Roger Fisher and William Ury, in their national best-seller *Getting to Yes*, point out that "learning one another's language" is especially important if we desire to benefit from our conflicts. They write: "The ability to see the situation as the other side sees it, as difficult as it may be, is one of the most important skills a negotiator can possess." If we want to see the situation as the other side sees it, they continue, then we must focus on our opponent's *interests* rather than his *position*. To illustrate this point, let's go back to my date with Cindy at the posh hotel.

Cindy's *position* was this: "Will, would you please plan ahead on events like this, and bring enough

*delay of game*

money?" As long as I focus on this position, I am likely to be defensive. My tendency is to think of all the other things that I did *right* on that date, and then to label her as critical for focusing on my one blunder.

However, if I look past her position and focus on her interests, then I might hear Cindy's real message: "Will, the *best* way for you to make me feel secure and to show me your love is to devote your energies to strong, organized leadership."

If I ask, "*Why* does Cindy want me to plan ahead more?" the answer is simple. In Cindy's upbringing, her father was a superb and decisive leader of the home. One of Cindy's strongest impressions of her father is that he demonstrated his love for his family by planning ahead and taking care of details. It might be true to say Cindy equates love with leadership. When I try to understand her interests rather than her position, the message I receive in the situation at the hotel is not one of attack, but one that says, "Will, please lead me so I can sense your love for me and, thus fall more in love with you."

Whether it's a Frenchman in football or a family in turmoil, if the desire to break down the communication barrier is *not* a top priority, true acclimation to one another will never occur. The following story, however, illustrates what can happen when two people finally become bilingual.

## *The Bum and the Beauty Queen*

Recently in my office I faced a husband and wife who in twenty-five years had not yet learned to speak each other's language. They were as different as a bum and a beauty queen. Although they could hear each other's words, they struggled with the meaning behind those words.

Lloyd was not actually a bum, though judging by his dress one would never guess he was one of the top stockbrokers in Denver. His wife Lana, on the other hand, dressed immaculately. If she were a pie at the county fair, she would win a blue ribbon just for looks. Lana was not a snob, nor was she particularly trendy, but her parents had taught her that one's appearance said much about his or her character.

Her attempts for years to get Lloyd to dress more sharply were met with hostile resistance. "You're always trying to change me," he would say. "Why didn't you just marry someone else if I'm not good enough for you?"

Lloyd's biting comments devastated Lana, and she resolved to keep her opinions to herself. But this lasted only until the next time she was embarrassed by his appearance. Then their cycle of fighting was repeated.

Hidden from Lana was the fact that Lloyd inwardly was very insecure. His memories of growing up were marred by cruel nicknames and dateless school years. Because of his chronic acne, his peers called him "Waffle Face." The self-conscious insecurity followed him all the way to college, where he tried to bury it with impressive achievements: He was elected fraternity president and student council vice-president, and made the dean's honor role and the varsity tennis squad.

Despite his laurels, Lloyd had never been able to shake the "Waffle Face" stigma. He always felt like a nobody, a loner, a bum, and, consequently he felt obliged to dress like one. Subconsciously he felt that to dress up carried with it the dangerous possibility of drawing further attention to himself—the last thing he wanted to do. So even as an adult—with many friends, a beautiful wife, and a lovely family—Lloyd still played the part of the bum.

Lana, meanwhile, was raised in poverty in a run-down housing project in Atlanta. Her father, though poor, possessed a wealth of self-esteem. What he lacked in money he made up for in integrity and pride. His home was always clean and warm. He made sure his wife and Lana, their only child, had enough to wear even if their clothes had to come from church ministries for the needy.

This sense of pride was passed on to Lana before her father and mother were tragically killed during Lana's sophomore year in high school. The memory of "Daddy's pride" gave her courage to make it through those lonely foster home days and to finish high school when many of her classmates were dropping out. She eventually won a scholarship to Tulane University, where she majored in accounting. There she met Lloyd, during their senior year. They immediately fell in love and were married less than a year later.

Within another year, their marriage was on the ragged edge. The problem went further than Lloyd's unfashionable dress. Lana was upset with Lloyd's refusal to show pride of ownership for just about anything. They owned fine cars that were never clean. Their home was expensive, but Lloyd did nothing for its upkeep. Lana felt she could never be proud of the man she had married.

Lloyd was equally discouraged, if not more. All his life he had lived in a prison called rejection. Through hard work he had reached dizzying heights on the corporate ladder, yet he still had not found the key to unlock his dreary cell of insecurity.

Finally the day came when Lloyd and Lana realized they were foreigners speaking different languages. In a counseling session in my office, Lloyd began to pour out to Lana the pain of his past. He was sobbing, his shoulders rising and falling with each heave. Lana sat alone at one end of a couch, stunned and silent.

Then Lloyd stood. The successful businessman in his mid-forties was shaking as he spoke. "I am not who you think I am," he cried. "And I can never be who you want me to be." Then he sank to the couch and, with his face buried in his palms, wailed like a child: "When will somebody love me for *me?* I want to be Lloyd; let me be Lloyd!"

The following forty-five minutes witnessed a beautiful and revealing meeting of two strangers who were both eager and afraid to share their lives with each other. Surprisingly, Lana had known little of Lloyd's lonely past. He had been too ashamed to talk about it with her. Lloyd was equally uninformed of Lana's childhood, a situation reinforced by the fact that she had no surviving family members to serve as links with her past.

Lana wanted to be proud of her husband in the same way she was proud of her father before he died. Lana's asking Lloyd to dress nicely or to care for their home was the desperate plea of a woman who wanted her love for her husband to survive and flourish. Lloyd, however, interpreted her requests as accusations of his inadequacy.

Each was speaking a language the other didn't know. They thought all along that they were fighting over clothing or clean cars or manicured lawns, but actually it was about cruel nicknames, crushed egos, and a gentle, loving father who was missed greatly by his daughter.

Lloyd now realized that Lana loved him and had married him despite his flaws. He recognized that he had misinterpreted her requests as rejections, when they were actually pleas for him to help her regain her love and respect for him. At the same time, Lana saw that she had been asking Lloyd to do things that were virtually impossible because of his shattered self-esteem. She accepted the fact that it would take Lloyd a long time to feel comfortable improving his appearance. If it meant regaining her love for her husband, however, she was willing to wait.

The bum and the beauty queen were reunited, because they stopped long enough to understand the feelings behind the messages, to hear the meaning hidden in the words, and to learn each other's language.

Is there a foreigner in your home? Maybe he sits across the table from you at breakfast each morning. Perhaps you go to bed with her every night. You might even wave goodbye to him every day as he boards a school bus. Let me ask you: How fluent are you in that foreigner's language?

## *The Final Play*

Let's return a last time to the huddle. This time bring your spouse and family along. Nothing's changed: Five seconds remaining, and your team is on the five-yard line, down by three points. You can win with a touchdown.

Knowing the game's outcome depends entirely on what happens in the next few seconds, you confidently call the final play. In the huddle, nodding heads reveal the fact that each player's greatest desire is to be part of the team and to move the ball into the end zone.

You break the huddle with a unison clap, and line up. What follows seems to happen in slow motion: The ball is snapped. A break appears in the defensive line, and you dive through to pay dirt. Victory is yours. You and your family celebrate in the end zone with high-fives and back slaps.

That could be the picture as you and your family face another honest-to-goodness conflict. It could be another

in a long series of team victories—rather than another instance of coming up short.

Once again:

Avoid "Delay of Game" by
actively listening to one another
and by learning one another's language.

# 5

# Backfield in Motion

*Don't bring up the past.*

"BLUE! NINETY-EIGHT! Blue! Ninety-eight!"

"Salty-dog left!"

"Hot tamale! Hot tamale!"

"Banana-in! *Huuuuuut!* HUT!"

Have you ever wondered what the quarterback is really talking about before the ball is snapped? Sounds like a grocery list to me. But these are not edibles...they're called "audibles." Calling them out is what the quarterback does after he fails to make up his mind in the huddle. The huddle breaks, the team steps up to the scrimmage line and the quarterback finally decides what to do. He figures he ought to fill in the rest of the team, so he "audibles."

Sportscasters love audibles. "He's audibling again! Can you believe it? That's the fifth time this series!" With all the excitement, you would think the new phone books had just arrived.

Audibles have a way of causing commotion. A wide receiver standing on the left side of the line suddenly hears the quarterback telling him he's supposed to be on the right side. So he takes off. The fullback is told to shift left. So he obeys. The assistant coach is instructed to pick up a coney dog for the tight end. And the head coach is pacing up and down the sideline wondering if the play will begin before the clock runs out.

No wonder so many time-outs are called in the game of football. A guy can get tired with all that movement out there.

In football's early days, you didn't see so much "motion," as they call it, going on before a play. In 1938, coach Clark Shaughnessy made "motion" famous and used it effectively at Stanford. With the invention came a need for new rules to govern "motion." For instance, it was decided that only one player could go in motion at a time, and all his movements had to be parallel to or away from the line of scrimmage. It was also decided that once a running back gets set in the backfield, he cannot move toward the line of scrimmage until the ball is snapped. If he does, the infraction is known as "Backfield in Motion," and his team is penalized.

In family conflicts, you're guilty of Backfield in Motion when you support your case by digging up things that should be left in the past. Backfield in Motion makes your spousal conflicts resemble courtroom battles: One of you is the prosecuting attorney, bringing forth every piece of evidence you can find, while the other cringes as the wide-eyed defendant:

"Well, what about the time *you* wrecked the station wagon back in August of '79?" shouts the prosecutor, jugular veins threatening to explode. "What do you have to say for yourself?"

"Well, I, uh..."

"Exactly! I didn't think you had anything to say!"

If you're like me, you don't enjoy being put on the witness stand. Your defensive walls quickly go up and you either counter with your own case, or else plead the fifth amendment and retreat into stony silence.

Evidence from the past may help win a case in a court of law, but it only clouds the issue in a marital or family conflict. Digging up the past is Backfield in Motion and we severely penalize ourselves whenever we violate this rule.

Three things are helpful in breaking the Backfield in Motion habit:

1. Together, clearly define the issue that led to the conflict.
2. Throughout the conflict, stay singularly focused on that present issue. Don't let yourself stray to other issues.
3. If other issues come to mind during the conflict, put them on hold and resolve them individually at a later time.

It is true that sometimes issues from the past come up because they have never been properly resolved, in which case you should together decide on a time to resolve them. More often, however, I believe a past issue reappears because we want to use it to our advantage in the present conflict. Whenever that's the case...let it go.

Backfield in Motion is valuable only in the court-room. It doesn't work in football or in family fights. So remember:

> *Keep it present!*

# 6

# Unsportsmanlike Conduct

*Give your opponent a sporting chance.*

UNSPORTSMANLIKE Conduct is a catch-all term for various sports violations. Punching an opposing player and throwing a ball at the referee, for example, are two easy ways to earn a penalty for Unsportsmanlike Conduct.

Similarly, there are a number of ways to commit this violation in a family conflict, as reflected in this list (I'm sure you can think of more):

- Over-generalization
- Apologizing prematurely
- Using "You" statements rather than "I" statements
- Poor eye contact
- Poor body language

## Over-Generalization

*Everyone* is *always* over-generalizing, it seems, when it comes to family fighting!

I recently counseled a family whose members were especially prone to over-generalization. Here's what I heard in the span of twenty seconds:

> *Dad* (to son):    You *always* seem so arrogant in the way you communicate with us around the house.

>      *Son*:    What do mean, arrogant? I'm not always arrogant. How come *everyone always* says I'm arrogant?

>    *Mom*:    I don't say you're arrogant. Do you ever hear me say you're arrogant? I *never* say you're arrogant!

> *Dad* (to wife):    But honey, look what position that puts me in. I end up the bad guy when you claim that you never say he's arrogant. You *always* make me look like the bad guy.

This may seem exaggerated, but it actually took place. In reality it is quite easy to fall into the trap of over-generalization. Isn't it usually true that when we conflict with someone, our eyes are blinded to the good things about that person? Therefore, we only see the bad. No wonder it seems to us as if that person *always* offends us or *never* does what we ask of him or her. But I am certain no one in the world is wrong, or offensive, or negative, or disobedient, or belligerent, or whatever, one-hundred percent of the time.

## The Hottest Picnic Ever

I once worked for an employer once who was an example of the fact that we don't have to fall into the overgeneralization trap. During my six summers working for Joe at a Christian athletic camp, I learned much about proper conflict resolution. I'll never forget one occasion in particular when Joe had to confront me over an issue.

At the time, one of my responsibilities was to ensure that provisions for an event known as "Cabin Night" were neatly packed into boxes and distributed to each cabin. "Cabin Night" was a sort of a indoor picnic, and the provisions included food, firewood, kerosene, matches, and so on.

I noticed one day that we were a tad short of kerosene. Now, I figured this was not a major problem since I knew where to get my hands on a little gasoline. All I needed to do was fill the jars and mark them clearly with the word, "GASOLINE." The counselors of each cabin would figure it out and take the necessary precautions. No problem, right? Wrong! When I learned later that several cabins were nearly incinerated, a sick feeling came over me. Why did I do such an idiotic thing? Then I thought: *Oh no! What will Joe do when he finds out?*

The word of my mistake spread quickly around camp, and soon Joe found out and summoned me. As I trudged to his office I felt like a condemned man on my way to the electric chair. I was certain that I would be fired on the spot.

To my surprise, Joe began our conversation by affirming everything he could think of about me. He praised my creativity, my ability to plan fun activities, my spontaneity, and on and on. For fifteen minutes he built me up before even mentioning the reason he had called me into the office.

Even though I knew it was coming, when he finally spoke of his anger over the gasoline incident (and believe me, he was angry), I didn't feel that he was attacking me. He told me that what I had done was extremely foolish, but I still felt like he was on my side. Joe could have easily over-generalized and said something like, "Will, you *never* seem to think before you act! When will you realize that your job requires you to be responsible?" He didn't say that, though. He thought long enough about me to remind himself that I was a valuable asset to the camp. I kept my job that summer, and the remainder of my time under Joe was phenomenal.

Joe is the director of the foremost Christian athletic camp for young people in America. He has learned sensitive battle skills that have allowed him to conflict positively with members of a staff that each summer numbers several hundred. His efforts have paid off.

Can we speak as glowingly of our own conflict management at home? Imagine what our homes would be like if, when we fought, our goal was to focus on the good qualities of each other as well as the bad!

The next time you are about to use the words "always" or "never" in a conflict with your spouse or your children, why not follow Joe's example? Remind yourself of the person's positive qualities. Remember:

> *Avoid over-generalization.*
> *Conflict resolution is more likely*
> *when we focus on the positive*
> *as well as the negative.*

## Apologizing Prematurely

Can you see why apologizing prematurely is unsportsmanlike? Imagine that that you and I are in a conflict. If I apologize prematurely, I haven't given you a sporting opportunity to share your grievances with me. In essence, I force you to bury your feelings and opinions. Why would I do this to you? Maybe I'm afraid of the conflict becoming too heated, or perhaps I don't want to risk being shown that I am wrong. Whatever the case, real resolution will probably not occur if I say "I'm sorry" too soon. That's unsportsmanlike!

## "You" Statements, Poor Eye Contact, and Poor Body Language

A quick way to close the lines of communication and prevent conflict resolution is to begin your sentences with the word *you*. This guarantees that your opponent will close his or her spirit and ears to you for the remainder of the conflict, and possibly much longer. "You" statements simply don't work well in a conflict. In order to break the "You" statement habit, learn to use "I" statements. Here's how:

1. Examine the feeling behind your accusatory "You" statement. Were you hurt initially? Were you feeling guilty? Resentful? Abandoned? Usually, some primary negative feeling underlies our reacting with a "You" statement.

2. Express this primary feeling with an "I" statement rather than attacking with a "You" statement.

3. Adopt a tentative approach.

4.   Ask the other person's help in resolving the conflict.  Very few people become defensive when asked for help.

*Example:*  Alice was hurt when Bob worked an extra hour at the office and arrived home late for dinner.  She wants to confront Bob, but she doesn't want to put him on the defensive.  What should she do?

1.   Get in touch with how she feels.  By the time Bob gets home for dinner, Alice is probably angry, but originally her feeling was one of hurt.  Almost always, hurt is the primary feeling that underlies the secondary feeling of anger.

2.   Express the hurt feeling in a non-attacking way and without using "You" statements.  For example: "Bob, I'm feeling hurt tonight because I feel second-rate whenever it seems that you make your job a higher priority than me."   Alice is tentative, not accusative, in saying that it "seems" as if Bob is placing his job above her.

3.   Ask for Bob's help:  "Bob, I don't like feeling hurt by you, and I definitely don't want my hurt feelings to grow into angry feelings.  Could you help me out by coming home for dinner on time or by letting me know in advance that you will be late?"

You may be saying, "I've tried this approach over and over with my spouse.  He (or she) seems to be fairly receptive to my words and promises to make amends, but nothing seems to change."  At times even the best of conflict resolution techniques do not work—usually because old habits have become too entrenched and the scars run too deep.

Sometimes when one spouse is repeatedly hurt by the other, the spouse who is doing the hurting must be held accountable for his or her actions.  I mentioned earlier the book *Love Must Be Tough* by James Dobson. This book was Dr. Dobson's revolutionary response to the commonplace advice of the day that told the hurting spouse, "Hang in there. Wait it out. Things will get better." This was especially true in Christian counseling circles. However, if you are the wife or the husband of a partner who does not respond to conflict resolution techniques, such as the ones found in this book, but rather who seems bent on destroying you and your marriage, I suggest that you read and think about *Love Must Be Tough* rather than what appears in this chapter.

On the other hand, if you and your spouse and children are committed to loving each other but simply don't know how to fight right, then read on. Begin to practice "I" statements right away with each other at home.

However, this is more difficult than it sounds. Our tendency is to say, "I feel *like...*" or, "I feel *that...*"—but when the words "like" or "that" appear directly after the word, "feel," we can be almost certain that the next word will be, "you." Rather than giving a tentative expression of his feelings, the speaker has only disguised a "You" statement. The effects on the hearer are the same—a closed spirit and closed ears.

We need to practice saying, "I feel _____", filling in the blank with the feeling that we are experiencing at the moment. It may help to purchase a thesaurus and become familiar with new ways to express the different shades of emotion that you may experience. For instance, various degrees of hurt include feeling "rejected," "in despair," "hopeless," "crushed," "broken," "wounded," and more. If you determine to quit using "You" statements and to give honest "I" statements, most people will respond to you in a non-defensive manner.

Poor eye contact and poor body language are also indicators of Unsportsmanlike Conduct. However, some-

times these are merely evidence of the individual's lack
of understanding of how much he or she communicates
with the eyes and the body. It is unsportsmanlike to discuss a disagreement or offense with another person while
refusing to look at him. Poor eye contact makes the opponent feel as if he or she was trying to fight a stone
wall. In my case, my tendency to keep my eyes focused
above the five-foot-two mark is an example of Unsportsmanlike Conduct. It drives Cindy crazy, and it never
moves us any closer to resolution.

Similarly, our body language during a conflict speaks
much louder than our words. Studies indicate that we
communicate with our bodies about eight times as much
as we do with our words.

How might poor body language be unsportsmanlike?
Imagine that Rick and Gina are fighting. Rick, with arms
folded and body turned away from Gina, says, "Okay.
You're right. I'm sorry."

Gina, reading Rick's body language, senses that he is
still closed to her. So, she decides to pursue the issue.
"Rick, something still seems to be troubling you. Let's
talk about it."

Rick, in a classic unsportsmanlike move, then says,
"Get off my back, Gina. I said I'm sorry, already. What
more do you want from me?"

Actually, what Gina wants is for Rick's body language to match his verbal language. Rick's words said,
"I'm sorry," but his body reflected the resentment that
still remained within him. He then appealed to his verbal message to make Gina look like the unforgiving
party.

If you want to take inventory of your eye contact and
body language, then the next time you are talking with
someone, ask yourself, "What are my eyes and body
communicating to this person?" You don't have to wait

for a conflict to arise to practice good eye contact and body language. Start today with the people around you.

> *Having a good fight requires "I" statements, positive eye contact, and positive body language.*

# 7

# Unnecessary Roughness

IT WAS EARLY FALL, the beginning of another promising season for standout quarterback Jim McMahon of the defending Super Bowl champions, the Chicago Bears. But in a game with Green Bay, a Packers defensive lineman charged into the Bear backfield and body-slammed McMahon to the turf long after the whistle had blown to end the play. The Green Bay player was fined severely, but that was no consolation for McMahon, sidelined with an injured shoulder for the rest of the 1986 season.

That was one of the most flagrant and injurious of Unnecessary Roughness violations that have marred professional football over the years. But far more tragic are the personal attacks and character assassinations that embitter many family fights. Unnecessary Roughness of the verbal or physical kind is no stranger to many families, and it hurts deeper and longer than the hardest body slams in the NFL.

Gary Smalley writes that one of the key causes of verbal abuse is found in the different way men and women view the words that come from their mouths. A man can spout a harsh phrase or critical remark and think nothing of the damage that might be done. For him, his words carry no more weight than a tiny pebble. However, the woman feels the heaviness of those words and experiences them as a gigantic boulder. How do you talk to your spouse? Your children?

Fathers, do you pick out character or performance flaws in your children, and then harp on those flaws, thinking your words can't possibly hurt? I'll wager that your children experience those words as huge weights. Husbands, have you ever drawn your wife's attention (for the forty-seventh time) to her vanishing waistline, thinking you were doing her a favor by frequently motivating her to lose weight? Guess what? She's not motivated. In fact, she's *de*-motivated by your Unnecessary Roughness.

And how about you wives? Do you know exactly the right words to say that will awaken your sleeping husband and teach him just how irresponsible he is? It doesn't work because it is Unnecessary Roughness. The roughest thing you can do to a man is to verbally attack his ability to lead responsibly.

Verbal roughness has no place in a marriage or a family, at any time. It is absolutely unnecessary. We'll study the destructiveness of the tongue in a later chapter when we look at God's perspective on anger and conflict. But for now, it is enough to say that if you can master your tongue, then you are probably a self-controlled person. And if you are a self-controlled person, conflict resolution will be much easier for you.

Commit yourself to not violating the Unnecessary Roughness rule with your spouse and children. Ask yourself, "What things do I commonly say around my family that could come across as unnecessarily rough?"

Any word that decreases another person's sense of significance or love could be called unnecessarily rough—even the use of seemingly harmless nicknames.

## *Words that Hurt*

"Hey, Dumbo! You look like a taxi going down the street with your doors open." As a youngster, I often heard words like these. I was the embarrassed owner of ears that were of epic proportion. Although my child-size head eventually grew into my adult-size ears, I carried the scars of those rough words for years. I was twenty years old before I felt comfortable with a haircut that showed the slightest part of the lobe. Words hurt—I'm sure you know it from your own experience.

It's a great temptation to violate the Unnecessary Roughness rule when we fight. Bob Bennett, a favorite Christian songwriter of mine, sings these words in one of his songs:

> Words, like weapons,
> Ask no questions as they kill.
> People, wounded,
> Once dancing, now are standing still.

How true! Our words have the power to stop a person dead in his or her tracks. I can't count the times I have listened to couples immobilize each other with destructive verbiage. After such a verbal assault the couple is never any closer to conflict resolution. In fact, they have widened the gap between themselves.

Why do we hurt each other with words? Are our vocabularies so narrow that we must resort to name-calling, swearing, ridiculing, and more? No, it's not that we're short on words. The problem is that we use especially rough words in hopes of winning a conflict—which, as I said earlier, is a vain accomplishment anyway. If you set out to win a conflict, you always lose in the long run, and the loss is all the more tragic if you are unnecessarily rough.

## *Hands that Hurt*

Sometimes physical roughness invades a marriage or family. This is particularly destructive because the victim of such abuse feels threatened at the most basic level of his or her security. Losing one's sense of significance is one thing, but losing one's sense of safety, especially in the very place where one should feel most safe, is devastating.

Recently I met with Rhonda and her son, Bobby. I knew from the moment she approached my secretary's desk and looked around for assistance that she and her boy were members of the "walking wounded." Bobby clung tightly to his mother's tattered overcoat, his small-er than average four-year-old body pressed firmly against her leg as if he would have loved nothing more than being completely absorbed by her—and hidden from the world.

"Please come in," I said. Rhonda and Bobby positioned themselves on the couch. Rhonda sat stiffly with her arms folded and her jaw tightly set. When I offered to let Bobby sit on my lap during our conversation, as I often do with young children, he immediately declined. Without once taking his eyes from me, he leaned his head against his mother's side and assumed a silent, watching manner.

"He's just shy," his mother offered. "I was like that, too, when I was his age."

Somehow, "shy" was not the word I would have picked to describe Bobby.

"We're here because we're leaving, and I was told you could help us find a place to go," Rhonda said. She said shelter homes had not allowed her and Bobby to move in "because they're too full, and they said we aren't in a life-threatening situation."

Rhonda reached up with her right hand and smoothed back her hair. I noticed a small bruise on her temple. I glanced at Bobby, noticing for the first time similar signs of abuse.

Rhonda said her husband's attacks had been seen and reported by neighbors, "but nothing's ever done." She told of an occasion when her husband punished Bobby for letting the dog out of their yard. "He made Bobby bend down and kiss his shoe, then he kicked him." She said a neighbor saw the incident and telephoned authorities—but again no action was taken.

"Nine years is enough," she said. "We aren't going back."

"You won't have to go back," I assured Rhonda, but I had little else to say. The damage had been done.

Because the shelters couldn't take them, we arranged for Rhonda and Bobby to stay with a family in our church. I watched as they left the church that day, Rhonda's torn coat flapping in the August wind and Bobby's little body blending into hers. *What will become of them?* I wondered. *Where will Rhonda be ten years from now? What type of man will Bobby grow up to be?*

## The Sad Facts

Physical abuse is rampant in our nation. In 1985, throughout the Denver metro area, 21,706 crisis calls were received by womens' shelters concerning physical abuse. The numbers have risen since then. According to the 1982 Crime Act, fifty-five percent of murders are perpetrated by relatives or personal acquaintances of the victims; seventeen percent of these homicides take place within family relationships. Statistics show also that employee absenteeism due to physical abuse results in an estimated economic loss to the nation of at least of three to five billion dollars annually.

So, when one family hurts, we all hurt. When one individual violates Unnecessary Roughness we all are violated. And the problem, being generational, is not easily subdued. One help agency for abusive men reports that at least eighty-five percent of men seeking services have been abused as children.

Although a fuller look at physical abuse is beyond the scope of this book, I do have a few suggestions for those who have encountered this crisis. If you are the perpetrator of physical abuse, seek help now. Many cities have groups for abusive individuals (such as AMEND—Abusive Men Exploring New Directions—in Denver). If you are the victim of physical abuse, don't waste another moment hoping your partner will rehabilitate. You can play a part in actively turning around the situation. First and foremost, if you are in present danger, seek refuge through your church or through a local women's shelter. In Denver, I recommend a ministry called Crossroads in Faith. I also suggest that you read *Love Must Be Tough*, by Dr. James Dobson, and *Women Who Love Too Much* by Robin Norwood. Both books can help you understand the role you may be playing in the abusive relationship and how you can stop playing that role. The first book is written from a Christian perspective, and the second is not.

Most of our Unnecessary Roughness is in the verbal realm, but sometimes even the gentlest of people are tempted to lash out physically. If you are the parents of young children, you probably understand how easy it is to react physically when your nerves are frayed by the demands of your little ones. A pediatrician friend of mine deals regularly with the heartache of child abuse. He advises the parents of his patients to always talk with the child before disciplining him or her. What this amounts to is the old adage: "Count to ten before you act." Even in adult conflicts we should heed this rule. Anything that sidetracks Unnecessary Roughness is a worthwhile conflict resolution tool.

Unnecessary Roughness of verbal or physical nature is a major roadblock to conflict resolution. It is one of the hardest roadblocks to overcome because of its lasting scars. Even if you determine to never be unnecessarily rough with your spouse or children again, you must be prepared to accept the fact that your poor track record will follow you for quite some time. Trust that has been broken through abuse is not easily restored.

We must all recognize that:

> *Unnecessary Roughness*
> *—either verbal or physical—*
> *quickly and easily tears apart*
> *a marriage, a family, and a nation.*

Football players usually bounce back from the bumps and bruises incurred due to Unnecessary Roughness. Healing and restoration can happen as well in families that have suffered similar blows. If your family is one of them, my prayer for you is that you'll bounce back as well.

# 8

# Too Many Players on the Field

Don't drag in outsiders

A FRIEND OF MINE recalls an exciting event from his college days at the University of Kansas: The Jayhawk football team was playing in the Orange Bowl. As the game neared its end, Kansas needed a score to win. Just as the clock ran out, the team pushed the ball into the end zone for a touchdown. But the celebration by the elated KU fans was short-lived. A referee's yellow flag lay in the middle of the field. The violation? Too Many Players on the Field. The penalty nullified the last-second score.

Dejected, the team and their fans headed back to the plains of Kansas with no victory...all because of a single moment when one player too many joined the game.

At Texas A&M, on the other hand, the tradition of the "twelfth man" on the field is welcomed. In 1922, the Aggies were playing Centre College in what was then called the Dixie Classic football game, forerunner of the Cotton Bowl. The underdog Aggies were whipping Centre at halftime, but the grueling first half had taken its toll on the A&M team. There were so many injuries that Coach Dana Bible was worried about whether he could finish the game with enough players.

He called for advice up to the press box, where a young man named King Gill happened to be sitting. Gill had earlier been on the Aggie football squad, but now was playing for the A&M basketball team. The basketball coach had told Gill not to play football anymore. Without a second thought, however, Gill dashed down, exchanged his street clothes for an ailing player's pads, trotted over to the sidelines, and with a smile let Coach Bible know he was ready and willing to play.

Gill didn't play that day, although he was the only man left on the bench when the game ended. The Aggies held their first-half lead, and won the game, 22-14. But Gill's willingness to help out, even at the cost of losing favor with his basketball coach, left a mark on the university's entire sports program. To this day at A&M football games, diehard Aggie fans stay standing for the entire game, symbolically waiting to be called to come on the field and help the team, and by their show of support giving motivation to the athletes who *are* playing.

So, you see, an extra man on the field, whether real or symbolic, can be either a blessing or a curse.

## The In-Laws

The saying goes that on your wedding day you marry an entire family, not just your husband or wife. This can be good and bad. Much like the Aggie players must feel inspired by their fans' support, there is nothing like having supportive in-laws backing you in your marriage, especially if you're newly married. I sincerely enjoy the company of my in-laws. Fishing or playing golf with my father-in-law is actually quite painless, and few people are as huggable as my mother-in-law, affectionately known as "Dodo".

But not all in-law relationships are this congenial. In fact, some of them exhibit family feuding of Romeo and Juliet magnitude. In these relationships, the young lovers are constantly being advised by their hovering parents on all manner of topics, starting with whether or not they should have married the other person in the first place.

In conflict resolution, the over-involvement of one's parents—or other family members and friends—is a violation of "Too Many Players on the Field". Such an involvement can often be the actual cause of conflicts.

Many conflicts are born in the first place because of over-involved outsiders. And yet many newlyweds readily welcome these extra players onto the field.

## Kate and Brian

Kate and Brian were engaged to be married while both were still in their teens. Neither had completed school, and Kate was living with her parents after having lived away from home only briefly. Although they had been going steady for seven years, they were sensible enough to know that marriage is a far cry from dating, and decided to come for premarital counseling. *This will be fun*, I thought—*a couple young enough that they haven't had time to develop a tangled web of problems.* But I was wrong!

Theirs was a classic example of Too Many Players on the Field. It didn't take long for me to realize that almost all their conflicts involved both sets of parents in some way. Sadly, in spite of the pain it caused, both Kate and Brian seemed to welcome their parents' involvement.

During the early stages of our counseling, Kate and Brian began to look for a house to move into after they were married. Kate's idea was to purchase a cute little house that needed a little fixing up. By coincidence, there happened to be one that fit that description just a few blocks from her parents' residence. On the other hand, Brian wanted to close a deal on a duplex in another neighborhood. It just so happened that Brian's brother was going to be a co-owner of the duplex and was willing to make the down payment for Kate and Brian. Brian's parents also thought the duplex was a great arrangement.

Kate and Brian soon began to clash over the housing issue. Because both were still trying to gain parental approval, neither was able to make a decision devoid of parental involvement. Sadly, instead of starting a fresh search for a house by themselves, Brian bought the duplex and Kate was forced to move into a home in which she felt completely uncomfortable. The effects of "Too Many Players on the Field" had already begun to mark this young couple, and they weren't even married yet.

In every sport there are limits on the number of participants playing at one time. When this rule is broken, it is generally because of some oversight. But in a marital conflict, where the number of players should be limited to two, the violation of Too Many Players on the Field is rarely an oversight. It is almost always a deliberate choice of the spouse who fears the loss of approval by a parent, a sibling, or a friend.

Before marrying each other, a man and woman must agree to establish their own traditions, plan their own vacations, choose their own place of worship, make their own decisions regarding the discipline of children, and so forth.  Norm Wright often asks engaged couples this question during premarital counseling: "Where do you plan to spend your first Thanksgiving?"  Dr. Wright wants each couple to begin thinking of themselves as a separate entity from their parents.  New couples have the freedom to make their own choices, and whenever they keep the proper number of players (two) on the field they save themselves much pain.

Each new couple must also choose to resolve their conflicts without dragging their parents, or anybody else, into the issue.  "Running home to mother" should be forgotten as an option.  If an impasse is reached in a conflict, it is wisest to seek the counsel of an unbiased third party, such as a pastor or marital counselor.

Here are three common ways we break the rule of Too Many Players on the Field:

1. Appealing to parental opinions or preferences to support one's case in a conflict.
2. Giving in to the temptation to share the "dirty laundry" with an outsider, such as a parent or a friend.
3. Drawing one's children into the middle of a spousal conflict in an effort to "beat" the other person.

When will we realize that our parents, our friends, and our children are not pawns we use in an effort to win a fight?

Recently I spoke with a man who was going through a painful divorce.  Because I knew both him and his wife, I was even more saddened by the news of their upcoming split.  Even sadder was the fact that their two-year-old daughter was being dragged into their battle.  The wife was insisting on sole custody of their child as the only option in their divorce agreement, and was refusing to let her husband see the child. "I can hardly believe my wife would be this vindictive," he told me. "I feel she is just trying to pay me back for all her past hurts, and she's doing it by putting our daughter between the two of us."

Broken marriages are always devastating, but when children are used as weapons in the process, it's the worst case of Too Many Players on the Field.

> *Leave outsiders where*
> *they belong . . . on the outside!*

# 9

# Piling On

Manage your stress.

WHEN ISAAC NEWTON discovered his "Second Law of Motion," he didn't know his work would have an effect on the National Football League centuries later.

Newton found that the greater an object's mass, the more difficult it is to speed it up...or slow it down. In the early days of football, players and coaches wondered how to stop eleven mammoth players, together weighing more than a ton, from landing on the opposing team's ball carrier all at once. They decided a rule with a penalty for its violation was in order. And thus Piling On became an infraction.

I marvel at those tiny gridiron "scatbacks" who defy the laws of physics and common sense. But I fear for their lives whenever I watch them play. The rule prohibiting "Piling On" is their saving grace. This rule prevents any player from jumping on another player after the referee's whistle signals that the play is over. And that's good news to a 180-pound running back who already has four other guys on top of him.

## *Under the Pile*

Newton's law, $F = ma$ (Force equals mass times acceleration), means nothing to most of us. But like the diminutive ball player, we all understand what it feels like to be "under the pile."

You and I live in an age of stress. Instead of working for a living, we live to work. Round and round we go like hamsters on a wheel, stepping off only to eat and sleep. And even our sleep is fitful and fraught with bad dreams.

Stress is fueled by fear. I am afraid of not having enough material goods, so I buy more. I am afraid of not making enough money to pay for what I have, so I work more. Now, I'm afraid my spouse is suffering from neglect, so I decide to relax more. Unfortunately, I have forgotten how to relax and my family says I'm no fun anymore. So, I buy them all new snow skis and promise to take them on a trip this Christmas if we can afford it—which means I have to work more. The pile keeps growing.

Are you under it?

## *Stress Creates a Mess*

All work and no play makes Jack a dull boy, and I might add, a lousy fighter too. But excessive work is not the only cause of stress. Other common stress inducers are getting married, a new baby, the death of a relative, the loss of a job, buying or selling a home, finishing a degree, and so on. So, you see, many things make up that pile you are under...and not all of them are bad.

However, stress, whether it's created by positive or negative circumstances, is the cause of many messy fights. And with every shovelful that you add to the pile, you are burying your chances of having a good family fight.

## *The Light of Day*

If you are a parent in a stressed-out family, then you must first realize that you have a problem on your hands. And like the muscle-bound lineman with a head of steam, your problem will not easily be brought to a halt. Remember…the greater the mass, the harder it is to slow it down. However, there are some things you can do to lighten the pile:

1.  Assess your stress! Take a look at the pile you are under and determine what factors are contributing to your stress.
2.  Discern which factors are within your control and which are not.
3.  Notice the factors that are within your control. Do you spend a proportionate amount of energy on each, or do some get more attention than others?
4.  Determine to achieve balance in the amount of time and energy you give to the things on your pile.
5.  Eliminate anything that needlessly takes your time and robs you of the energy you could be giving to your family.
6.  Finally, do not add more to your pile until you have crawled out from under it and breathed some fresh air for a while. In other words, learn to say *No*.

These are obviously broad guidelines within which only you can decide what should stay and what should go. In many instances the decision is already made for you. For example, there is very little you can do to escape the stress caused by a death in the family. It is out of your control. But there are a multitude of things you *can* control...and you must control if you want to have successful family fights.

I have found that I deal best with stress when I strive for a balance in these four areas:

1. Mental
2. Physical
3. Spiritual
4. Social

As multi-faceted creatures, you and I think, feel, play, pray, mingle, and much more. When we devote too much time to one area, another area suffers. For instance, we wear out our "thinker" by over-working and our "player" screams for attention.

My job requires a truckload of mental stamina. Sitting all day and working with people and their problems is at times burdensome. When the burden increases, usually the first things to suffer are my physical exercise and my social relationships, including the time I spend with my family. Consequently, my body, my family, and my friends are all upset with me...and rightfully so. I have cheated them.

Cindy and I have had some of our most unprofitable fighting during these times when I let myself get out of balance and under the pile. After a long day of counseling, not only do I lack the energy to exercise and socialize, but I also lack the energy to fight fairly. At these times I slip back into my old style of conflict, and I break all the rules.

Above all other needs, I believe, is the built-in desire

you and I have for the spiritual. We have a deep longing for a relationship with someone higher than ourselves. When we do not nurture this relationship daily, this too brings stress—a far deeper stress than any other. And stress creates a mess in family fighting.

Unless people rearrange their priorities and achieve a balance, they will remain under the pile. But if you're

*piling on*

like me, you get things like this done only when you schedule them on your calendar. Each of my counseling appointments is important to me. But it wasn't until I began seeing that my devotions with God, my times on the basketball court, and my evenings with family and friends as equally important appointments that I finally penciled them into my schedule and brought my stress under control.

Now I notice that when I've met with God, nurtured my body, and played sufficiently, I am a far better fighter. I am kind and gentle during conflicts. And I have energy to go the distance if it is a particularly long one.

How about you? How long has it been since you've poked out your head from under your pile, and seen the light of day?

# 10

# Goal Tending

> When a conflict occurs, the
> interests—the goals and desires—
> of each participant must be valued
> and considered equally.

I'M SIX-FOOT-FOUR, and although I'm no Kareem Abdul, my basketball shots are rarely blocked. It has happened, though—and on one occasion by a woman.

One summer afternoon at the camp where I worked, I was playing basketball with several other guys when Jeri asked if she could join our game. Relieved that she was on the other team, I even acted a little condescending toward her when I realized she would be guarding me.

"Don't worry Jeri. I won't go full speed," I said reassuringly.

"That's okay," said Jeri, "I'll just try to keep up with you."

*This is going to be great*, I thought. *I might even set some sort of camp scoring record.*

For my sake I'll spare you the details of what happened. But had I known that Jeri was a starting guard for the Louisiana Tech women's basketball team, and was nicknamed "the Ragin' Cajun," I might not have bothered even to play that day. Jeri blocked my shot *three* times that afternoon, and I resented her more each time.

Jeri's treatment was nothing, of course, compared to what would happen if I ever tried getting shots past the arms of NBA professionals. An increasing number of players top the seven-foot mark, and block shots at

*goal tending*

will—some without ever leaving the ground. To prevent these giants from totally dominating the game, a rule against "Goal Tending" was established. It simply states that once the ball begins its descent toward the basket, an opposing player may not block it. This prevents the tall players from camping under the basket and slapping away every shot that comes in their direction. When a player commits Goal Tending, the other team automatically is awarded two points. I like this rule, because it gives the "little guy" a chance.

We can be guilty of Goal Tending in our family conflicts when we try to block one another's goals. Usually, the bigger and more powerful family members do most of the blocking.

Here's an example: Sixteen-year-old Jeff wants to stay out two hours past his usual curfew this Friday night because his high school is having its homecoming game. All his friends are staying out later and Jeff doesn't want to be different. But Jeff's father is reluctant to let him drive the family car late at night, and he is also wary of the party that Jeff would be attending after the game. Therefore, without any discussion, he vetoes Jeff's plans. As the person with the power in the household, Jeff's father knows he can block his son's goals at any time...and he does just that. He is guilty of Goal Tending, and the result is that he has earned Jeff's resentment.

Whenever goals are blocked during a conflict, so are the lines of communication. (You can bet that Jeff won't be interested in talking to his father for a long time.) Think about your own family fights. How often has a family member offered an opinion or revealed an interest only to have it slapped away?

The picture becomes one of both sides racing back and forth, up and down the court, each trying to score points with verbal shots at an imaginary hoop. But again and again the shots are rejected. If your family is at fault in this area, then blow the whistle.

I know of only one way to stop Goal Tending when you fight with each other. When conflict occurs, the interests—the goals and desires—of each participant must be equally valued and considered.

## Story-Boarding

When I began writing this book, I sat down with my publisher and a few other friends and went through a process called "story-boarding." Conceived by Walt Disney and his assistants, it's an approach to creative planning that allowed the Disney team to turn acres of Florida fields and citrus orchards into a gold mine called Disney World. Many people thought Disney was foolish to attempt such a feat. But that didn't bother Walt. He simply allowed his creative team to dream big. In Disney's mind, no idea was a bad idea. The same applies to solving family conflicts. Once I realized that, I was astonished to discover how effective story-boarding can be in family counseling.

The first step in story-boarding is identifying the challenge or the problem that needs solving. The Disney team's challenge was to create a successful theme park. The challenge facing me was to write this book. A typical challenge or problem facing your family might be trying to establish a curfew for your oldest teenager that everyone will feel comfortable with. He wants a later curfew, while you as his parents believe the present curfew is just fine.

Once the sides are taken on an issue like this, our tendency is to hunker down in our own foxhole and defend our position to the death. "I demand a later curfew!" versus "We won't let you have it!" This approach to conflict doesn't work because the side with the strongest firepower always wins. The losing side, meanwhile, retreats to load up with heavier artillery for the next battle.

But in a more successful family fight, both sides must come out of their foxholes and meet on the middle of the battlefield. Once you have abandoned your positions, then begin to listen to one another's interests. A good tactic is to write down together all the reasons—the desires and goals involved—for each position. For example, what are your older teenager's desires and goals in wanting to have a later curfew? And, as his parents, what are your interests—your desires and goals—in wanting to keep the present curfew? Take a look.

| *Why I want*<br>*a later curfew:* | *Why we think*<br>*your curfew should*<br>*not be changed:* |
|---|---|
| 1. All my friends have a later curfew, and I want to be treated as maturely as they are. | 1. You'll be too tired to go to school the next day. |
| 2. When the game or any other school event ends, that's usually when the fun is just beginning, but I have to come home. | 2. We're not comfortable with the activities that go on after the games. |
| 3. I'm the oldest kid in the family, yet I still have the same curfew as everyone else. That's not fair. | 3. We don't think you will have the time or energy to get your homework done. |

Can you see that both sides have legitimate interests and concerns? No sixteen-year-old wants to feel left out or different from his or her peer group. And what parent wouldn't question the activities of many teenagers? It's understandable that an oldest child would want to hold some privileges that single him or her out as being more responsible than the younger children. Likewise, it's common for parents to be concerned with how the oldest child is handling such responsibilities as homework. But after considering the interests and concerns listed above, Mom, Dad, and son are much better equipped to discover solutions and alternatives than they would be had they held tightly to their positions and fought from the foxhole. Here's a possible solution that could be settled on:

Because so many sports and social activities occur on Friday night, Mom and Dad agree to relax son's curfew on that night. However, this new privilege has one condition: He must inform his parents where he will be and what type of activity he will be attending. If his parents discover that he has been dishonest in reporting to them, he will lose the Friday night privilege temporarily. In addition, he forfeits the Friday night privilege if he repeatedly fails to do his homework during the week. Finally, the son will receive additional new privileges (such as more time on the phone) that will distinguish him as the oldest child.

You will be surprised how much easier compromise is when you discuss interests rather positions. And when story-boarding is used to help indicate those interests, usually everyone is satisfied with the result. If you decide to use story-boarding, you will find yourselves doing more listening and less blocking of each other's shots. Fewer blocked shots, meanwhile, means more victories for you and your family.

# 11

# American Tourister

IN THE SUMMER after I closed my high school books forever, the Cunningham driveway was opened nightly for "P-I-G" and other basketball contests. Dinner was barely over when Rusty and Rob drove up first, in time to sweep the June bugs off the court. Then Peter would appear in his beat up set of wheels we dubbed the "Gangstermobile."

"Say, man...your mom got any cookies tonight?" he'd ask, as the "pump, pump, pump" of vinyl on pavement began.

Next came Pat and Van, and finally, Bart.

Dad's privet hedge was out of bounds, as were the side of the house and the imaginary line between the cars and the elm tree. A sorry shot frequently landed in the tomato plants beyond the fence, where retrieving it meant risking the escape of Liza, the family mutt. "Open that gate very slowly, Rusty, cause if you don't..." It never failed. Liza would be halfway down the block before we could catch her and resume our game.

We played until the sun was tucked in bed—nestled under the blue sheet and the purple blanket and the ink-black comforter with the silver sequins. The last cookie was eaten (usually by Bart), and the first crickets began their song, signaling the end of tonight's games. Goodnights were spoken, high-fives exchanged, and my friends were off into the night.

My vivid memories of those times include the nicknames that rang out in the evening air. Lanky Rob was the "Dunk Monster." Peter was the "Air Hose." And I was dubbed "American Tourister" because I "traveled" so much.

## *Traveling*

"Traveling" is one of the most embarrassing penalties in the game of basketball. It's like dancing alone before hundreds of onlookers at a party. The player with the ball who takes one step too many without dribbling, forfeits possession of the ball to the other team. "Tweet!" the whistle blows, and the referee spins his arms to signal the call. The player turns red, and the crowd heckles: "Way to go, Jones! Take a suitcase next time!"

But traveling isn't restricted to the hardcourt. Spouses all over the world are penalizing their marriages by committing this violation. When a conflict arises, they travel...right out the door. Instead of hanging around long enough to resolve the problem, they turn their back on their opponent and walk away.

I was a champion traveler in the early days of my marriage with Cindy. Conflict had always been uncomfortable for me. When the fight got too tough I found it easier to walk away. But my actions left Cindy feeling insecure. How was she to know where I was going, or when I was coming back?

It's heartbreaking for me to look back now and to think of Cindy crying as I stalked out the door, turning my back on the woman I courted and asked to marry me. I am ashamed to admit I ever treated her this way. But I did. Fortunately, I've curbed my habit of traveling over the years, but Cindy's hurt from those earlier violations did not disappear easily.

What about you? Do you leave your spouse high and dry when conflict becomes difficult? Do you walk out on your kids when you are fed up with them? Do you take a hike when your parents don't see eye-to-eye with you? Do you hit the road when it looks like you are losing in a conflict? If so, ask yourself if your leaving will move you closer to or further away from resolution. If your answer is "further away," then commit yourself now to not walking out.

You may be asking, "What if I am losing my temper in a conflict? Do I hang around and make matters worse by my angry presence?" There is a time and place for a proper time-out. As we discussed in the chapter on "Off-sides," sometimes when you feel a conflict is getting out of hand it is best to agree with each other to take an intermission, and then return to the issue later for resolution.

Sometimes one of the persons in a conflict becomes so angry that he or she cannot even discuss the option of taking a time-out. If that's the case, then the other party who is less angry should say that since what is needed is conflict resolution, and since the other person's anger is preventing progress toward resolution, a time-out is needed. After saying, "The conflict can be resumed later," the person who is not angry should walk away until the atmosphere for discussion is calmer.

## A Long Way from Home

A pastor friend of mine jokingly tells of a time he walked out during a conflict with his wife. They were driving home one Sunday with their two children after eating out. As they talked, what began as a minor disagreement between two people who normally are best friends grew into a larger struggle in which both spouses felt dishonored by the other.

The wife was driving. "Okay, stop the car!" my friend told her. "I'll walk home from here. Just stop the car," he repeated.

His wife slowed the station wagon, then came to a halt on the shoulder, as she had been ordered. The kids watched in disbelief from the back seat as their father got out and began walking.

He pictured it for me this way:

"Here I am—walking along the highway trying to prove a point. My kids are hanging out of the window, crying and pleading for me to get back in the car. My wife is hugging the shoulder, creeping along at two miles an hour while hundreds of cars are whizzing by—many of them no doubt driven by people from our church. Suddenly it occurred to me that we were about ten miles from our home.

"Needless to say, I got back in the car."

You might conclude from my friend's story that "traveling" in a conflict can be comical. But a better point from this story is that it can leave you lonely, embarrassed, and a long way from home.

So please understand:

> *"Traveling" only delays resolution.*
> *But if tempers become too heated,*
> *agree to take a time-out. Then,*
> *resume resolution attempts*
> *at a mutually decided upon time.*

## Don and Meagan Revisited

In chapter one we discussed Don and Meagan, the couple who were too afraid to unwrap the gift of pain, and who consequently suffered through six marriages. After so many failures, Don and Meagan came to me for counseling. They wanted to give marriage one more try. Both of them believed they could get it right this time. I asked them why, after so many false starts, they were willing to try again.

Their answer was ironic: "We've fought more with each other during our engagement than we ever did in all of our previous marriages combined...and we've never been happier."

What an incredible statement! Can you imagine someone banking the success of their seventh attempt at marriage on the fact that they fought so much? That's like two people crediting their happiness to their incompatibility. But I believe Don and Meagan are closer to achieving a happy marriage than are the majority of couples who remain faithful to each other but who refuse to face their conflicts openly and to regularly bring them to resolution.

Do you want a happy marriage? Do you long for a

joyful family atmosphere? Take a tip from Don and Meagan who spent years walking out in the middle of fights. "Traveling" is not the answer. In fact, it only opens the door for greater conflict down the road.

In his marriage seminars, Gary Smalley tells couples that one of the keys to a happy family is the cultivation of "shared mutual conflicts." He is usually referring to some shared experience like a raft trip down the Colorado River or a wilderness campout, in which the couple together faces and overcomes difficult circumstances. But I believe we can view the circumstances of our typical conflicts at home in the same way—being committed to face them together for the sake of a stronger relationship:

> *Conflict that is mutually and successfully navigated always builds a relationship. Conflict that is avoided eventually returns to destroy a relationship.*

Driveway basketball at the Cunningham house was never void of injuries. Someone was always catching a knee in the thigh, or an elbow to the cheekbone. And every night tempers flared. But no one ever took the ball and went home. Why? Because we were friends, and we knew that conflict could be expected in a well-played game. If things got heated we might take a cookie break to cool off... but we always resumed play.

I hope you can see that walking away in the middle of a conflict will result only in a penalty for your family

The next time you're tempted in a conflict with a loved one to "take your ball and go home," stop long enough to look around you. You *are* home! Now, hang in there and make the most of it.

# 12

# Checkmate

End a fight with an act of love!

*CHECKMATE!*

No other game concludes as regally—or abruptly—as does chess. The picture I get is of two dueling swordsmen, one of them driving the other into a corner. Suddenly he strikes away his opponent's sword, and it falls to the cobblestone. The victor's blade is swiftly poised against the the loser's Adam's apple. Touché!...Checkmate!...the pieces go back in the box.

There are no overtimes, no extra innings, no tie-breakers—just one word, and it's over.

Not so with most sports. Nor is it true, unfortunately, in most family fights. If you've ever wrestled with the problem of how to end a conflict, you know what I mean.

On several occasions I have counseled couples who couldn't seem to bring a fight to an end. After weeks of talking through the problem and even coming to the conclusion that the problem was resolved, they still felt uncomfortable with each other. "How do we end it?" I hear frequently. "How do we start feeling good about our marriage again?"

Ending a fight is particularly difficult. Unfortunately, I know of no decisive words ( like "checkmate") that give

113

an unmistakable signal to everyone that the conflict is over.  Even "I'm sorry" often comes short.  However, Cindy and I have discovered something that works for us and I want to share it with you now.  I call it, "Check (your) mate".

## The Potato Chip Principle

While I was attending seminary, Cindy and I lived in a small apartment near the campus.  We loved our little place and Cindy did a wonderful job of decorating it, but over the years, we became increasingly aware of how cramped it was.  For instance, my desk, where I did most of my studying, was right in the middle of our living room—not an academic atmosphere.

One night just before the Thanksgiving break, after a long day of classes, I forced myself to stay up late to work on a theology paper.  Cindy cheerfully offered to keep me company.  Right then I should have smelled trouble.  Her happy tone of voice said one thing:  "Will, what I'd really like us to do is spend time talking.  And I'd prefer that you weren't studying while we did it."

I was determined to work on my paper, but accepted her offer to stay up with me.  I opened my books and began to read.  Cindy settled on the sofa next to me.

Then it happened.

"Honey," she began, "What kind of bread do you think I should bake for Thanksgiving?"  She had that sort of dreamy look she gets after spending an hour browsing through *Country Living* magazine.

She continued:  "Should it be honey-wheat or sesame-seed?  Or maybe I could make potato bread.  I don't know.  What kind do you want, Will?"

"Potato bread's fine, dear," I said, without looking up from my book.

Silence.

"Well I haven't made honey-wheat in a long time. How about honey-wheat?"

"Honey-wheat's fine, Cindy." This time I looked up at her, then quickly dropped my eyes back down at the book, hoping she would catch the message. *Please God. Make her go to bed*, I thought.

Apparently, God didn't hear me. Cindy continued: "I've been having trouble with my baking since we moved to Colorado. I guess I should use the high-altitude wheat flour."

I was starting to lose it.

"Or maybe," she said, "there's something wrong with the oven. Do you think it's the oven, honey?"

That was it. I lost it.

"Cindy—make honey-wheat, make sesame-seed, make potato, make anything, but please–go to bed!"

More silence.

Then tears.

Then two hours of discussion and apologies and, needless to say, no studying. Finally we resolved the matter, but we both still felt lousy.

Then Cindy did an amazing thing. She got up from the sofa and went into the kitchen. Soon she was back, and in her hands was a small bowl filled with my favorite snack—potato chips. She gave me a kiss on the cheek and she went to bed.

Checkmate! The game was over, and we were both winners.

Do you see the principle? "Check (your) mate" means simply this: When you've done all you can to resolve a conflict yet still feel lousy, go back and *check your mate*. In other words, don't just leave him or her high and dry. Check to see how he or she is feeling, and accompany this check with an act of love (that's the important part!). When all the words have been said, an act of sacrificial love is the necessary, final move to bring about resolution. It's the bowl of potato chips that says, "Truce." It's the back rub that says, "Everything's okay."

It's the last move on the board that says, "Checkmate...I love you."

# 13

# MOSCOW

EVERY CHRISTMAS SEASON a barrage of games and toys explodes onto store shelves across America. (This is not hyperbole; some actually do explode.) When I was growing up, kids were satisfied with toy machine guns that *looked* like machine guns. We still had to provide the sounds (which, by the way, have been misrepresented for years in comic books with words like "Rat-a-tat-tat"; but the real sounds, as well the neat sounds *we* made in imitation, were too difficult to spell). Today, toy companies provide everything but the bullets.

But every year a few toys with redeeming qualities restore my faith in Santa as someone other than a radical arms distributor. I am speaking of those trendy board games (I call them "mind games") that have captured the hearts of the baby boomers. These games require ordinary people to answer extraordinarily difficult questions like: "If you ruptured your spina bifida, with which would you be least inclined to make an appointment—a neurologist, a paleontologist, or a plumber?" I have found that "Pass" is usually the best answer for me.

The complexion of American recreation has long been in need of a face-lift anyway, so the appearance of these mind games is a welcome event. And I would be foolish to overlook the rules of these games and the manner in which they might contribute to this book. Actually, this type of game has only *one* important rule: All the contestants must commit themselves to *think*—which is exactly what most of us are usually trying to escape when we play games.

Recently I endured an entire evening of "thinking" with one of these games. My friends, in whose home Cindy and I were guests, said it would be fun. All it did was cause us marital trauma.

This particular game requires you to convey a word to your partner (without talking) by drawing clues on paper. Your partner has to guess the word within one minute. "Oh, let's be partners, Will," said Cindy. "I think all the spouses should be partners." "Good idea," chimed the rest of the group. I was skeptical.

The game started and the word on the card I selected was *Moscow*. With a white-knuckled grip on my pencil, I waited for the minute-glass to be turned over. "Ready. Set. Go," said our hostess.

I took a deep breath and started. First, I drew a tree on the left side of my paper. Then, hanging from one of the branches, I scribbled a clump of Spanish moss.

"Moss!" Cindy shouted.

Only fifteen seconds had elapsed. I thought, *This is easy*.

Next, I drew what was obviously a cow on the right side of the paper, and I looked at Cindy.

She thought for a moment. "Um...dog!" she guessed.

I smiled, and pointed to the cow's horns.

"Ummm...a goat?"

The timer showed twenty seconds left. My anxiety was building. I quickly drew a circle around my cow, thinking that would help.

"A horse!...A buffalo!...A deer!...An antelope!"
Cindy was running out of animals. And I was frantic.
Finally she hit it. "A cow!"

I nodded my loudest "YES!" Now all she had to do
was put the two together. I pointed back at the moss.

"A tree!" Cindy shouted.

Time had run out...and so had my patience.

moscow

Our evening as partners spiraled progressively downward until it was time to leave. We hardly spoke a word to each other on the way home. I was still holding a grudge over *Moscow*.

The problem in this situation was clearly mine. Do you recognize it?

The game required us all to do one thing…that was *to think*. Naturally, every person thinks differently. But throughout the evening I was expecting Cindy to think like *me*…and blaming her when she didn't. In reality, my wife is sharp as a tack, and probably the best elementary school teacher I know. And yet, I am ashamed to admit, with each comment or disgusted look I was telling her I thought she was unintelligent.

If you want to learn to have a good family fight, then ignore the way I acted toward Cindy on that dreadful evening and remember this:

> *To have a good family fight you must stop demanding that other family members think the same way you think.*

## The Chocolate and the Peanut Butter

Your spouse is not your clone! Your wedding was not a celebration of the "Vulcan Mind Meld," where your two brains sort of blended together to form a single unit. Rather it was an event at which two players agreed publicly to function as a team, neither being more important than the other. That is why at the end of the ceremony the preacher said, "I now pronounce you husband and wife," instead of, "I now pronounce you…*You!*"

Some of the most delightful things in the world are actually the combination of two quite different components. Reese's Peanut Butter Cups are, in my opinion, the hallmark of this principle. You'll never find the two ingredients—chocolate and peanut butter—battling over top billing. Instead, they work as one. Because of their confectionery compliance, they are enjoyed by people all over the world.

Perhaps in your marriage, you are the chocolate and your spouse is the peanut butter. You can expect, therefore, that as long as you live together you will each think differently. Accept it, and move on.

I have counseled couples who have been married for close to a half century, and still they have not accepted each other's uniqueness. I often wonder why they even bothered to get married in the first place. It would have been much easier to fall in love with a mirror.

Take a long look at your own spouse. Do you see him as he really is? Do you see her uniqueness, her enjoyable blend of qualities that in a special way are hers and hers alone? Or are you seeing—or trying to see—merely a reflection of yourself?

How about your kids? Do you accept the fact that they are not exact replicas of you? Or are you busy trying to change them to have your tastes, your views, your quirks? If you're trying to change them, you'll have about as much success as the chocolate would in trying to monopolize a Reese's Cup. And you'll look as silly as I did trying to get Cindy to say "Moscow."

Don't insist on renovating your loved ones. Rather, learn to enjoy each other's differences. Make it a lifelong endeavor to recognize and value the things that make each person in your family unique...and realize that achieving such respect for one another is no trivial pursuit.

# 14

# Fix Your Divots

> *Be willing to forgive.*

GOLF AND I do not get along. If you ask me, the game involves far too much precision.

There are times when I do everything right—my head is down, my backswing is slow, my left arm is straight, my club-face is closed, my eye is on the ball—and still I embarrass myself. I dribble the ball off to my right about thirty yards, where it chooses to roll under the only thorn bush on the course. I never reach the green before the people behind me get upset and start yelling.

Whether or not you play golf, a golfing rule called "Fix Your Divots" is worth mentioning here.

A swinging golf club can inflict an ugly wound on an unsuspecting putting green. These miniature craters are called "divots." Left unrepaired, they create a moonscape appearance. But golfers like to play on smooth surfaces, so—out of courtesy for fellow players—they fix their divots.

I have never actually done this myself because I have never caused a divot, but I have seen other men and women fixing them. They kneel on the turf and gently prod the grass back into position with a divot-fixer. The damage is repaired and the game goes on.

## *Family Divot-Fixing*

Sometimes in a family fight you must also repair the damage you've done before resolution can be achieved. Because you are human, you will not abide by all the rules for correct fighting all of the time. And when you break a rule, you hurt people—you put a divot in someone's life. Angry words, cold shoulders, false accusations, infidelity...all these can cause divots. Fighting fairly often requires you to humble yourself...to kneel down and fix your divots.

There is no better divot-fixer than forgiveness. It's the salve that heals when wounds run deep. It's the two-way street where "I was wrong" and "I forgive you" meet head on. In my counseling practice I have found that most of us have a much harder time with the second. "I was wrong" is chewable, but we gag on "I forgive you." Asking forgiveness is always easier than forgiving. But forgiving someone who has put a divot in your life is often necessary for resolution to occur.

I know no harder thing to forgive than infidelity.

I have known couples who have not even been married a year before one of the spouses is unfaithful. Generally, when I meet with such a couple, my primary goal is to accommodate the spouse who has been offended. Initially I do little probing to find out why or how the incident happened. I merely assume that the couple has a very large divot to deal with, and we don't need to spend a lot of time discovering why or how it got there.

I believe that when infidelity occurs for the first time in a young relationship, it should be dealt with immediately. When early infidelity is treated with strict confrontation, it has less chance of occurring again.

The treatment involves three steps. First, the offender must confess to the offended. "I was wrong" must be stated sincerely. Second, the offender must go through a sufficient period of restitution, which is determined by the offended party. During this restitution period, the offender party might be asked to obtain a written, clean bill of health from a doctor, or to agree to be involved in marriage counseling. The goal during this time is to reinstate value in the offended person and integrity in the offender. Without restitution, the offender is left feeling guilty and the offended is left feeling devalued and suspicious. Finally, at some point, the offended must say "I forgive you" and move on. I have seen couples go through this process and rebuild loving relationships.

I have camped on the subject of infidelity only to prove a point. Sometimes conflict resolution calls for plain, old-fashioned forgiveness. If one spouse can forgive another for something as painful as infidelity, there surely is no divot in your life so large that you cannot repair it. In fact, you must! If you continue to remind each other of old crimes, then you cannot learn to have a good family fight. But once you get past "I was wrong" and "I forgive you," you have an unobstructed shot at the hole.

*Kerplunk!*...Resolution!

# 15

# False Advertising

*Express your feelings truthfully.*

ON THE PLAINS of western Kansas is an eight-thou-sand-pound prairie dog. After years of passing the signs that advertise this freak ("Largest In The World!"), I final-ly went to see it for myself. I took the detour off I-70 and headed south.

I drove past farms and fields and tiny community churches, and I wondered what it was like to live in the shadow of such an awesome creature. I imagined a huge, hairy mammal with a single pair of giant, chisel-shaped incisors protruding from its upper jaw. I decided I would not feed it from my hand.

In the distance was a patch of tents surrounded by trees and chain-link pens—an oasis beckoning life's thirsty thrill seekers. Out in front of the establishment, sweating inside a little wooden booth, was Dusty, the ticket seller and tour guide. And there, ten yards away, was the main attraction towering twenty feet above the parking lot...eight thousand pounds of wood and chick-en wire and plaster of Paris.

In shock, I watched as mature adults handed Dusty their cash and credit cards. The queue of people stood at the impostor's feet and looked up as if it were Mount Rushmore or the Lincoln Memorial. I was ashamed of myself for being jockeyed into this ridiculous detour, but at least I didn't take pictures of the silly rodent. While shutters clicked and tourists oohed and ahhed, I turned my car right around and headed for home. Dusty's mouth was agape as I drove away. Maybe to him I was a bigger wonder than the fraud that loomed behind him. After all, I was also passing up the Russian boar, the six-legged cow, and the thirty-six inch, live donkey.

## False Advertising in the Sports World

False advertising can be funny when you observe it from a distance, but being duped by it is maddening. One moment the Olympic sprinter crosses the finish line and we herald him as champion. The next moment he fails to pass the post-race drug test and we boo him as villain. We feel we've been had, and we don't like it.

We expect integrity in the world of sports, and, in fact, athletic competition could not exist without it. When an athlete says he or she is drug-free, we believe the claim. When the promoter lauds an upcoming fight as "the battle of the century" we expect nothing shy of Normandy in the ring. A team steps onto the field or court, and has no doubts that the opposing team will send out the same number of players—no more and no less. A wrestler walks onto the mat, weighing in at 118 pounds, and he trusts that the man he faces will be in the weight range as well. A referee dons the black and white, and we demand that he be unbiased. Anything else would be false advertising.

## False Advertising and the Family

Family fights, like athletic contests, must also have truth and integrity. I am speaking particularly here of truthful expression of emotions. If you are mad, *say* you are mad. If you are glad, *say* you are glad. But don't say you're glad when you're mad. That's false advertising.

*false advertising*

We tend to feel the same about an emotionally dishonest opponent in a family fight as we do about the doped-up track star. Both have lied to us and we feel resentful.

Here's an example of the destructiveness of false advertising:

## *Ben and Lonnie*

Lonnie came from a family of nine children. Her husband Ben, on the other hand, was an only child. In Lonnie's house, if a person wanted to be heard, it was necessary to yell. Ben's home was more sedate. Lonnie's family fought. Ben's didn't.

As might be expected, after only a few months of marriage Ben and Lonnie were extremely uncomfortable with each other. Ben was distraught whenever the two of them had a fight. He hated fighting and did everything he could to avoid it. "Fine—everything's fine," was his standard answer if Lonnie sensed something was wrong and questioned him. Then he would retreat to the bedroom or bury his face in a book, blocking out Lonnie for hours. But his words and his actions didn't line up. He was hiding behind false advertising. Lonnie, meanwhile, felt something akin to what I felt when I discovered that the largest prairie dog in the world was nothing more than a cheap statue.

Fortunately, Ben was willing to admit his false advertising. He was also able to see how his background influenced how he fought—or, in his case, *didn't* fight—with Lonnie. He eventually accepted the fact that fighting is not necessarily a bad thing, and he and Lonnie went on to have some very successful fights. Perhaps the biggest change though, was that Lonnie no longer had to put up with Ben's false advertising. For the first time in their marriage, when Ben said he was "fine," Lonnie could believe him.

## *Emotional Management*

Can you and the members of your family believe one another when a feeling is expressed? Or are you guilty of false advertising?"

Every member of your family must be responsible for managing and expressing his or her feelings. You can help each other become better managers and expressers, but ultimately no one should be expected to read someone else's mind.

Avoiding false advertising in your family fights requires you to do two things. First, you must be committed to telling each other your real feelings in the midst of conflict. Second, once you have made this commitment, try to steer clear of blunt honesty. The truth does not always have to hurt. Choose your words carefully. Soon you will be fighting with truth and integrity.

I make the trip across western Kansas at least twice a year. The signs still advertise what I have come to affectionately call the Trojan Prairie Dog. But I don't trust signs like I used to, and I will always hate false advertising.

# 16

# Match the Hatch

*Woo your opponent*

"LOOK AT THAT GUY!"

"I know. Can you believe his wife lets him leave the house looking like that?"

"And he's a fat one, too. I wonder what he's been feeding on."

"Beats me. Whaddya say we head upstream?"

"I'm game."

If you're a fisherman and you've ever come home empty-handed…now you know why. Not only can the fish see you, but they also talk behind your back. And what they are saying is not nice.

Most fish consider humans to be "fashion nerds." From a fish's point of view, a camouflage jumpsuit only further reveals mankind's poor taste in clothing. And any intelligent fish knows that flies are for eating, not for pinning on a cap or a vest. Fishermen have given the entire human race a bad name in the animal kingdom. And I must admit that I am one of them.

I was indoctrinated into the sport of fishing when I moved to Colorado four years ago. I knew I was hooked when I was in the dentist's waiting room last month and

133

noticed I had picked up *Field and Stream* instead of *People* magazine. I have even gone so far as to read (shudder) *The Curtis Creek Manifesto*, a weighty tome with all sorts of tips for catching "the lunkers," "the hog-bodies," and "the Walters"—names for the fish you never catch, or even see, except on certain restaurant walls. And I'm beginning to wonder if those are anything more than chicken wire and plaster of Paris.

Anyway, there is a rule in the sport of fishing that should be mentioned in this book—the rule called "Match the Hatch."

Matching the hatch is a time-consuming procedure. It involves finding out what the fish are eating that day and then matching it with an artificial morsel that looks similar. Usually the smart fisherman will walk downstream, away from the "holding waters" where he intends to fish. Then, with the help of a screen, he will sift the surface of the water hoping to catch evidence of the *"carte de jour."* A bug, a fly, a tiny freshwater shrimp...any of these might be on the menu that particular morning, and the wise angler doesn't want to be caught serving the wrong thing.

This all takes extra effort, of course, but once you've matched the hatch you are way ahead of the other fishermen on the river. While they're dangling all sorts of unappealing baubles in the water, you'll be ringing the dinner bell...and catching fish!

To repeat: For catching fish, you gotta give 'em what they like. Just any old thing won't do. Start throwing in every lure under the sun and they'll swim on by faster than you can say "Zebco."

The same thing applies to a family fight. If you plow recklessly into your opponent, you'll most likely scare him or her away from what could have been a successful confrontation. But if you take the right approach—if you match the hatch—you can woo your opponent towards resolution.

## Fishing for a Fight

The next time you're about to engage in a fight—or better still, before the fight even has a chance to develop—ask yourself these questions: "What can I do to make this conflict appealing to my opponent? How can I prevent him or her from being scared off before we can achieve resolution?" Once you have decided on your approach, you are ready to make your first cast.

Over the years I have learned the proper bait to use with Cindy for luring her into a successful fight, and with hard work she has done a decent job of matching the hatch with me. I've found that before I say anything negative, Cindy likes to hear or experience something positive from me. So, I look into my tackle box and look for something creatively positive as my approach. Sometimes I'll wait a whole day before confronting Cindy about a particular gripe of mine. I'll be careful to fill that day with various things that build Cindy up—helpful tasks, well-timed compliments, surprise gifts—all are overtures I might use to prepare Cindy to receive my words later on.

I am amazed how many people have this process completely cattywhompus. They go fishing for a fight with all the wrong bait. Instead of wooing their spouse gradually, they botch things up with their bungling efforts, then expect to repair the damage with a card or flowers. My experience with fishing tells me, however, that it takes much more work to lure a fish back after it's gone than it does to keep it there in the first place.

## *Hook or Harpoon?*

A variety of lures and bait are available to the serious fisherman. Most have unappealing names like Wooley Worms, Shad Raps, and Stink Bait. The fish don't mind, though. They just wait for the right one to come along, then they gobble it up.

Similarly, though you may feel like using a harpoon instead, you can use many good methods to gently "hook" your spouse into a good fight. These, too, may sound unappealing to you because they require more of your time and energy. But a loving spouse will spend the time it takes to learn and choose the right approach for enticing his or her mate into a positive conflict.

*match the hatch*

# 17

# Wake-up Call

WE'VE BEEN IN THE WORLD of sports and games to learn about the right rules for family conflict. Perhaps as you read, there were some points or rules that, with a little further thought, could be easily and effectively applied in your family conflicts. Perhaps there is more benefit to be gained from these concepts, more truth to be applied in love in your relationships with the people who mean more to you than anything else on earth.

Stop for a moment now. Pinch yourself. It's time to wake up. This is not just ink and paper...this is reality.

Besides seeing that conflict can be beneficial, you've also read about the helpful rules listed below. Think about them again—about what they really mean for *you*:

1. *Pick the right time to fight.*
2. *Learn to listen.*
3. *Don't bring up the past.*
4. *Give your opponent a sporting chance.*
5. *Control your hands and tongue.*
6. *Don't drag in outsiders.*
7. *Manage your stress.*

8.  *Give value and consideration to the interests—the goals and desires—of each person.*

9.  *Don't walk out.*

10. *End a fight with an act of love.*

11. *Be aware of your differences—and accept them.*

12. *Be willing to forgive.*

13. *Express your feelings truthfully.*

14. *Woo your opponent.*

## *Another Box*

Now, reach a second time into the gift of pain and you will find another small box. Pull it out and observe it. Much like the box of rules, this one, too, has an inscription on its side, in gold letters: *Styles.*

We often use animals to describe destructive styles of conflict. "They were fighting like cats and dogs," we say, or, "It was a real hornet's nest in there," or, "Stay away from Dad today, he's a bear." And when was the last time you heard of a wet hen that wasn't mad? I suppose that, over the years, even the animals forgot how to play properly the game Fight for which the Governor gave them rules.

Unfortunately, we humans have adopted their bad habits. In the next section you'll learn what kind of "animal" you are, and which rules you have a tendency to break.

# part iii

# Styles

# 18

# What Kind of Animal Are You?

SOMEONE MAY HAVE said to you before, "I like your style." That person was not talking about your hairdo or your sunglasses or your clothes, although each of these lends to your style. He or she was talking about that mysterious combination of qualities—God-given and parent-taught—that make up "You." Change your hair, throw away your sunglasses, wear a toga, and you will still be essentially the same. And like the little boy in "The Emperor's New Clothes," someone will still recognize you for who you are—the same person with the same old style.

You have a style of fighting too. Every time you enter a conflict you take your style with you. If you want to learn to have a family fight without killing one another, then you need to take a look at your style.

Study the animal kingdom and eventually you will find an animal that fights like you do.

Animals tend to fight the same. A disgruntled bear is consistently unpleasant to be around. I know from experience that an enraged hornet can be counted on to chase you for blocks.    A wet hen is far less hospitable than a dry one.   And if you've seen one catfight or dogfight, you've basically seen them all.

You and the members of your family will tend to fight in a predictable manner also.   What kind of animal are you? Here's a story to help you find out.

### WHO WERE YOU IN THAT CANOE?

### CHARACTERS:

*Helmut* (the Turtle)
*Edge* (the Shark)
*Stinkwood* (the Skunk)
*Hyde* (the Chameleon)

It was a sweltering July weekend and Helmut was miserable.  He had tried everything imaginable to keep cool, but still he felt as if he were baking in his shell.  Suddenly he had an idea.

"I know!  I'll call up my friends and invite them to go canoeing with me."  Just the thought of a cold, rushing river made Helmut shiver with delight.

He crawled to the telephone as quickly as he could and dialed his friends.  Still the task took a long time, since turtles dial almost as slowly as they crawl.  But eventually he rallied his buddies and made all the arrangements.  Edge would pick up Stinkwood, and Hyde would take the bus from across town.  All three were to meet Helmut at the river where he would be waiting with the canoe.

Everything went as planned, and by one o'clock in the afternoon the four friends were drifting downstream on a wide expanse of crystal current.

"It doesn't get any better than this, guys!" said Stinkwood as he leaned against the stern and sipped a cola.

"Yeah. This is the life," said Edge.

Helmut was proud of himself for planning such a successful outing, and was just about to draw attention to this fact when suddenly Hyde screamed from the bow, "Rock! Look out for the rock!"

Up sat the other novice sailors just in time to man the paddles and steer clear of a mossy boulder jutting from the middle of the river. But a worse sight loomed ahead—a stretch of water white and churning, full of obstacles.

"You idiot!" snapped Edge, wheeling around to gnash his teeth at Helmut. "We're all going to be killed because of your bonehead idea!"

Helmut tightened his lips—and said not another word during the rest of the crisis, nor for the rest of the afternoon, for that matter.

Meanwhile Stinkwood was shouting to Hyde. "Do a J-stroke! "No, no! Now sweepstroke! Sweep! Sweep! Sweep! Oh it's too late," he continued furiously. "We're headed for that rock. Your sweep strokes are not good at all," he said swiftly, turning again to Hyde "I've been watching you the whole time and you're barely putting your blade in the water. The gunnel, man, the gunnel—at least reach past the gunnel. Get your hands wet for heaven's sake! Pull! Draw! Sweep! Backwater! Oh, I give up!"

Stinkwood finally stopped nagging long enough for Hyde to respond. "It's not my fault!" he said. "I've been paddling like crazy. Edge is causing our problems—look, he's ruddering on the wrong side. But I want to know why there weren't signs posted further back to warn us. Don't we pay taxes for that?"

Edge ordered Stinkwood and Hyde to shut up and paddle. Finally the little vessel made it through the flume, but not without minor scrapes incurred in its pinball journey through the rocks. The rest of the soda had gone overboard, but besides two broken paddles, nothing else was damaged—except Helmut's ego. Ever since Edge's scathing remarks, he had been silent and sulking.

The four friends continued their journey with Edge still fuming, Stinkwood still offering advice to Hyde, Hyde still blaming anyone and everyone, and Helmut silently vowing that he would never, *ever* speak to Edge again.

I ask you now…*Who were you in that canoe?*

## Developing a Style

Something about being in a canoe with another person seems to bring out the worst in all of us. (Ask Cindy—she and I have been partners before.) The same is true of living in a house with other family members. You don't have the option of changing partners in the middle of the rapids. But during those turbulent times we develop a style of conflict that helps us to either sink or swim.

Imagine your family on that same trip described above. When the smooth sailing turns into rough rowing, how do you respond? Whatever your answer is, that is your style. And that is probably how your family sees you every time a conflict arises in your household.

As children, we watch, we listen, we focus, we collect every tidbit of information that might be useful later. Part of what we gather are skills that will help us relate to others as we mature. Most often, we learn these skills from our parents or the significant others that helped raise us. These are our coaches. They teach us about laughter, sorrow, hard work, and play. They teach us about God, politics, cause and effect, and the value of money. And although they don't know it, with every squabble, quarrel, quibble, hassle, and tirade they teach us the conflict skills we will use for the rest of our lives.

I don't like to blame parents for every quirk that appears later in a person's life. Even in the most dysfunctional of families, the parents are not always the bad guys. But every young person's mind is like a computer. It stores in its memory banks all the data programmed into it, good or bad. As our coaches fight, we watch and we take notes. Later we use the same skills, and eventually we mold these skills into a style that is comfortable for us. Some of the patterns may be right and some wrong, but whatever is *familiar* and *comfortable* to us is what we retain. In short, each of us has a particular style of conflict that we think works best for us. Unfortunately, later in life, a style that is familiar can become painfully uncomfortable.

Many adults who were raised in an alcoholic family will admit learning early that the best way to handle conflict with their alcoholic parent was not to handle it at all.

They saw what happened to the non-drinking parent (or someone else) who tried to confront the alcoholic with his or her drinking problem. Verbal and physical abuse was often the result. Occasionally some of the alcoholic's rage was spent on the child, who—not understanding why he or she was the target of such rage—discovered that it was infinitely safer to avoid conflict with the alcoholic parent altogether.

Let's say that the child is a boy who eventually grows up to be a man. He marries his high school sweetheart. Soon the honeymoon is over and they stop putting their best foot forward with each other. Conflict begins. But because conflict is so painful for the new husband, he avoids these uncomfortable confrontations. He buries his own angry feelings because, from his experience, feelings have never been safe to share.

When he means "no" he says "yes." When he is mad he acts glad. And when he is hurt he says nothing. Soon he becomes so full of anger, resentment, and discontent that he begins to rebel against his wife. He stays late at the office. He stays out with the boys until all hours of the night. He ceases to do any work around the house. Sometimes he even explodes and lashes out at his wife in a manner all too similar to the way his father treated his mother.

What is the real problem with the way this young man handles conflict? The problem is that he is stuck—limited to one style of fighting that is getting him nowhere fast in his relationship with his wife. He is just like Helmut in the story above. He holds everything inside until he finally blows. If he does not change, he and his wife are headed either for divorce or for a very long and hurtful marriage.

## Jack and Jennifer

Jack came from an alcoholic family like the one described above. As a boy he frequently experienced the crushing blows and heavy-handedness of his father, who drank heavily. Jack also was stuck in a destructive style of fighting, having learned early that it was not to his advantage to argue or to express his opinions. He perfected the art of remaining silent.

People such as Jack who have an unresolved conflict with a parent often tend to marry someone whose personality closely resembles that parent. The marriage then becomes the continuation of that person's to resolve what should have been resolved long ago with his or her parent. While in college Jack married Jennifer, a bright young woman with a quick mind and a tongue that kept pace. She was also quite headstrong. Soon their marriage closely resembled the father-son relationship for which Jack held so much contempt. As conflicts arose in their household, Jack slipped into his quiet mode.

At one point in their marriage, Jennifer wanted to buy a home in a fairly secluded locale. Jack adamantly opposed the idea, believing the home was too expensive for their means, as well as too isolated. But fearing Jennifer's forcefulness, he backed down and they bought the house. Financial difficulties followed soon after.

Jennifer meanwhile wanted to have a baby. Jack was opposed. But instead of sharing his opinions, he adopted his sphinx-like attitude again, and soon she was pregnant. When their son arrived, Jack felt saddled with both a house and an infant that were unwanted and unaffordable.

Bitter conflict arose. Years of bottled-up anger came pouring out of Jack, and it was all directed at Jennifer whom he blamed for all his troubles. Jennifer withdrew into an isolated life of caring for their new son. Jack also withdrew, spending most of his home life weeding, mowing, trimming, painting, repairing, and all the other work required to keep up the dwelling that had become an albatross for him. He sought release by joining two softball teams, but the loneliness was unbearable. While other husbands stepped up to the plate to the sound of supportive family cheers, Jack played to the delight of no one. Whether he got a hit or struck out, the result was always the same—silence.

Who was at fault? Jack or Jennifer? In reality, both were at fault. A family or spousal conflict is never one-sided. But Jack's failure to learn how to express his feelings in a normal conflict was the primary cause of their problems.

Like Jack, are you stuck in a destructive style of fighting —and yet are unwilling to change? You do not have to come from an alcohol-stricken family to be stuck in a dysfunctional fighting style. I believe there are two major styles of dysfunctional fighting, and each of those two styles comes in two forms. We can describe them this way:

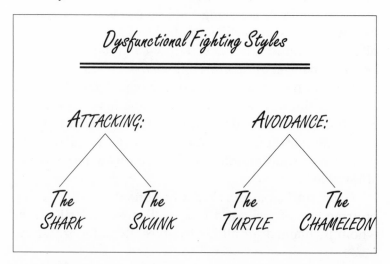

The following chapters should help you and your family members learn more about your own fighting styles. But first I want to encourage you with another story.

## *Getting Unstuck*

In the seventies, Hollywood threw my generation's next hero onto the silver screen. Instantly, Sylvester Stallone became an idol. And *Rocky*, his sleeper screenplay of the year, awakened audiences all over America. Soon hordes of Rocky "wanna-be's" were drinking raw eggs, lifting weights, and imitating Sly's gutteral voice.

As usual, one successful movie on the theme was not enough. Tinseltown followed with sequels, and I suppose the list will someday go like this: *Rocky I, Rocky II, Rocky III, Rocky IV, Rocky vs. Rambo, Rambo vs. Bambi, Rocky & Bambi Do the Rumba (in 3-D)*, and so on.

In one of those earlier displays of movie machismo, Rocky was training for his climactic fight with Apollo Creed. Rocky's trainer, Mick, kept forcing him to lead with his right hand instead of his usual left, to teach him to rely on speed rather than brute strength. The big Italian grumbled under his seasoned mentor's instructions—the awkward switch made him look like a rookie playground fighter.

In the final fight, following his trainer's orders, Rocky used his newfound right-handed style to advantage. The audience, the announcers, even Apollo himself were caught off guard. All had expected a lumbering lefty, not a lightning-quick right-hander. Of course, as in all of his movies, Rocky won the fight and we all left pumped up and several dollars poorer!

The conflict style we develop early in life is similar to the boxing style that a young boxer like Rocky develops early in his career.  Fortunately, just as in the illustration above, we can learn new styles that are contrary to our usual ones.  Learning a new style of fighting is awkward, and sometimes we will be tempted to resort to our old ways.  But it's refreshing to know we aren't doomed to keep our old style for the rest of our lives.

I hope you have begun to understand what sort of "animal" you are when it comes to conflict.  Your entire family will benefit from knowing each other's tendencies—you can remind each other to avoid your predictable worst forms.

Remember to help one another.  Each member in your family may have a distinctive conflict style, but you are all players on the same team, playing the same game.

Read on to learn more about your individual style.

# 19

# The Big Stinker

CINDY AND I were ecstatic when we bought our first house. At last the kitchen table wasn't forced to do over-time as a sweater rack, and the bathtub was used only for bathing and not for washing car mats. Hallelujah! We were free at last!

But one night, shortly after we had moved into the neighborhood, we were rudely awakened by the unmis-takable odor of skunk. The smell drifted through our open window, and seemed to just hang there inside our bedroom. Our new dwelling was not quite so rosy any-more. In time the smell faded. Unfortunately, the stink of living with someone who fights like a skunk does not disappear so easily.

## *The Skunk*

A Skunk makes a big stink about everything. The Skunk is not satisfied until he has raised his tail and squirted stink-juice over every issue that might cause a conflict with his spouse or other family members. The Skunk enjoys conflict—and the smellier, the better. Cross a Skunk, and you'll hear about it.

More traditional names for the Skunk are "nag," "shrew," "perfectionist," "picky person," and so forth. Do you know any Skunks? Or perhaps *you* are one?

Skunks often violate the Offsides rule. The Skunk

plows on ahead, spraying his opponent as he goes, unconcerned about whether this is the right or wrong time to conflict.

Similarly, the Skunk is a frequent violator of Delay of Game. The Skunk rarely stops to listen.

In fact, the Skunk regularly breaks all the rules, except that a Skunk is rarely guilty of walking out or of apologizing prematurely. You will rarely find a Skunk who backs down or who finds it easy to say, "I'm sorry."

Although I hesitate to label this as purely a woman's problem, I have found that women are attracted to the Skunk style more than men. My counseling practice verifies this. Sad, but true, women have been labeled as Skunks (or, more commonly, "nags") for as long as relationships have been around.

Why would anyone use such tactics in order to get their needs met? I found an answer not long ago in Robin Norwood's *Women Who Love Too Much*. This book tells how women, throughout history, have tried a multitude of methods to change their men in order to feel loved and to achieve a sense of value that was missing earlier in life.

It's common today as well, the author indicates. If a woman grows up with an absentee father, or a father who is abusive or an alcoholic or a workaholic, she will progress through life with a love-shaped vacuum aching to be filled. Her tendency is to try anything, or put up with anything, to cause a man to fill this vacuum. Ironically, in order to "win" the prize for which she has struggled since her youth, she requires a mate who is equally as distant as her own father. She becomes a Skunk in search of love. She pleads, nags, cries, threatens, gives in, and lavishes love upon her man, all in an effort to change him. And his response is to retreat from the smell.

As I read Norwood's book, I was disturbed by the assertion that this dysfunctional style of relating plagues women more than men. Why would men who grew up with distant or abusive parents respond differently than women? As a counselor, why did I consistently encounter couples in which the woman was the Skunk and the man was running from her spray? The Bible provides an answer.

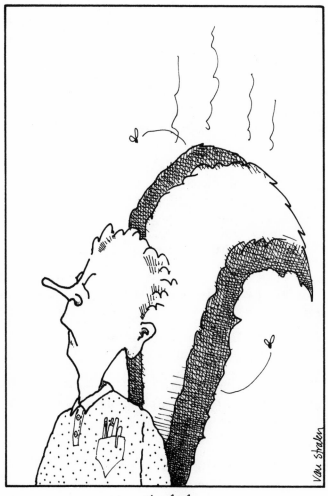

*the skunk*

## *The Roots of Skunkism*

The third chapter of Genesis succinctly provides an explanation for Skunkism. Here we begin to catch a glimpse of the Fall of mankind. The separation of creation from Creator, the discovery of nakedness and shame, the plunge into interrelational darkness—these were just a few of the consequences of Adam and Eve's rebellion against God. In the initiation of these consequences recounted in chapter three, the term "curse" is used. That curse reaches into all aspects of life, then and now, including our conflicts with one another and the manner in which we respond to them.

Listen to what God said to the man and the woman after their disobedience (from Genesis 3:16-19):

> To the woman He said,
>
>> "I will greatly multiply
>> Your pain in childbirth,
>> In pain you shall bring forth children;
>> Yet your desire shall be for your husband,
>> And he shall rule over you."
>
> Then to Adam He said, "Because you have listened to the voice of your wife, and have eaten from the tree about which I commanded you, saying, 'You shall not eat from it';
>
>> Cursed is the ground because of you;
>> In toil you shall eat of it
>> All the days of your life.
>> Both thorns and thistles it shall grow for you;
>> And you shall eat the plants of the field;
>> By the sweat of your face
>> You shall eat bread,
>> Till you return to the ground,
>> Because from it you were taken;
>> For you are dust,
>> And to dust you shall return." (Genesis 3:17-19)

After witnessing the birth of our son, Wesley, I recognize one of the inevitable elements of God's curse upon the woman. It just plain *hurts* to have a baby, as Cindy will quickly tell you. But some aspects of the curse in Genesis 3 still puzzle me. For instance, why would it be a curse for a woman's desire to be for her husband, as verse 16 implies? From a husband's point of view, that sounds like a bargain. However, when we link that portion of verse 16 with the verse's last phrase, the curse comes into plain view.

> "Yet your desire shall be for your husband,
> *And he shall rule over you."*

Here is a woman with an intense desire for her husband to love her. Some Old Testament commentaries describe this desire as bordering on disease (the Hebrew word translated here as "desire" stems from a word which means "to have a violent craving for a person or thing"). But the woman's desire is not satisfied. Instead of meeting her needs, her husband often withholds his love from her. In short, he holds a position of rulership over his wife.

I don't believe God's original intent in creating Adam and Eve was for one of them to rule over the other. That was a direct result of disobedience. This is the crowning blow of Eve's curse. Whereas the man and the woman once had perfect fellowship, now they have alienation and conflict. Their relationship, initially characterized in terms of oneness and suitability, now is described in terms of domination and unmet desire.

Put yourself in Eve's position. Imagine that you have an intense desire for Adam. You have a deep longing for your relationship to be as it once was. Yet Adam seems strangely distant, preoccupied with more important matters, such as his work. You have tried everything you

know to get him to respond to you, to come toward you,
but he only retreats, calling you a "nag". In essence, he
rules over you. He always seems to get his way, and you
always seem to lose. Here is the root of Skunkism. It lies
in a curse.

If you were to join me in my office during a typical
counseling session, you would see at one end of the
couch a woman desperately trying to get her husband to
show interest in her and the family. At the other end you
would see a man wholly devoted to something else—
typically his job. You might almost see the frustration
oozing from his furrowed brow. With arms crossed, he
complains that his wife and kids never appreciate anything he does and that they constantly place new demands on his time. In truth he is is a modern day Adam
sweating out his curse.

"I work hard, and look what I get!" says the man. He
wants fruit, but his pay is thistles. He views his wife as a
Skunk, and to some extent he is right. She does make a
big stink about many things. But she knows no other
way. How else can she gain the attention of a man who
is always away at work, toiling under the curse of his
labor? Hear me clearly: Many more women than men
are Skunks. But they don't want to be. Rather, they
know no other way.

Recently a man in a premarital class asked me, "Isn't
it true that in marriage most women have more demands
and expectations than men?"

"Yes," I answered. "But generally when a woman is
making demands, it is because her needs within the relationship are not being met in the first place and she
knows no other way to get her man to meet her needs."

## Skunkism: Nature and Nurture

By now you can see that Skunkism has two components. It is the result of both nature and nurture. Like disobedient Eve, the woman who labors under the Genesis curse feels unworthy of God's love. She then looks to a man to meet this need. Therefore, her nature is to be a Skunk, striving to control the love of a man. In other words, she has replaced God, the highest object of love, with a mere human being. And if she grew up without a nurturing father, she is doubly cursed. Her chances of being a Skunk are even greater.

You may be asking, "Is there a way out of Skunkism?" Yes there is! His name is Christ. And He is the way back to God. He alone lifts the curse. He alone makes the Skunk worthy of the Father's love again. And only He can heal the little girl (or boy) who has been making a big stink in order to gain human love. But you can do one more thing to rid your home of Skunkism.

## Taking Your Spouse off the Throne

As a Skunk, what do you expect of your spouse? If you look honestly at all your expectations, you will probably find that you expect perfection. Not only do you expect perfection, but you also frequently *demand* it! And we men are equally as guilty as the women in this matter. If you are a Skunk, you have taken God off the throne and replaced Him with a human being. But filling God's throne is too large an order for any human being.

Take time to list all your expectations of your spouse. It may help for you to think categorically. For example, what are your domestic expectations? Your financial ones? Your social ones? And so on. Once you have completed your list, decide to view these expectations as your "Christmas list."

When I make out a Christmas list I never expect to get everything on it. Otherwise I would view whatever I received as "given," not a "gift." The same is true in marriage. There are no "givens," no rules dictating that one spouse *must* do a single thing for the other spouse. So why continue to make a big stink about it? It is far better to accept the fact that only God can meet your needs totally. Learn to view the things your spouse does for you as a "gift" to receive and enjoy, not to demand.

Finally, don't stop voicing your expectations to your spouse. Make out your Christmas lists for as long as you live. But *do* leave behind all those smelly tactics of trying to force those expectations to be met. Once you quit nagging, pleading, crying, and threatening, you can relax in the thought that God loves you and will meet all your needs. And the times will indeed come when your spouse comes through with a gift from your list.

If you heed these words, you will be well on your way to dropping your destructive style of conflict. As a Skunk no longer, you will make your home a more fragrant place to live.

# 20

# Come On In; The Water's Fine

OCEANOGRAPHERS inform us that an enormous variety of sharks cruise the seas of our planet, and that most of them are nonaggressive, even docile creatures.

Such assurance from these scientists does little, however, to calm our fears of the fish we view as monsters from the deep.

Occasionally, just when we think it is safe to go back into the water, we are scared again by news reports of some horrid shark attack along some beach crowded with vacationers. The story is typically accompanied by a graphic picture of a surferless surfboard with a fifty-inch bite taken out of it. We joke about it nervously, but many of us are content to lie around on our beach towels rather than venture past the tidemark.

We watch the movie *Jaws* and say to ourselves, "Docile creatures, huh? These oceanographers must be on drugs."

## The Shark

If you live with someone who fights like a shark, you know how serious the casualties can be from an attack. The Skunk may make a big stink about everything, but the Shark moves in for the kill. And it's never a pretty sight. The Shark is a master of roughness.

If the shark is known for his sharp teeth, then the person who fights like a Shark is known for his or her sharp tongue. Verbal abuse (and sometimes physical abuse as well) is the Shark's trademark, and once the Shark gets started, it is not long before he has whipped himself into a frenzy.

Our friends the oceanographers indicate that most sharks will attack human beings only when provoked. This is true in marriages, as well. Most Sharks seem fairly peaceful until they get married. Suddenly, matrimony has allowed another creature into the aquarium, and the Shark begins to feel invaded—provoked.

Strangely, Skunks and Sharks seem to be frequent marriage partners. The Skunk provides the provocation, and the Shark takes the bait by viciously reciprocating.

The marriage of a Skunk and a Shark is a frightful union. If you've witnessed two spouses who are constantly attacking each other, you know what I mean. The Skunk is usually convinced the problem lies wholly with the Shark, because the Shark is "such a mean and nasty individual". Of course, the Shark blames the Skunk entirely: "I would not have to resort to this if my buttons were not constantly being pushed," says the Shark. In reality, provocation and retaliation are *equally* destructive. Both are attacking styles of conflict, and neither works well in a marriage.

## *The Roots of Sharkism*

Think back with me to the earliest biblical account of Unnecessary Roughness. Out of the crippled relationship between Adam and Eve came a son whose name was Cain. Like most firstborns, Cain was undoubtedly his parents' pride and joy. He was the original "only child," and perhaps Adam and Eve "spoiled" him thoroughly.

Then Abel had to come along and ruin everything. Not only did Cain have to share a bedroom now, but he had to share Mom and Dad too. Since Abel arrived, Cain felt his value had dropped significantly. He now represented only a fourth of the world's population rather than a third. Soon he noticed that even God paid a lot of attention to his pesky brother.

Yes, this new kid on the block was creating quite a

*the shark*

problem for Cain. He did his best to suppress his anger, but with each passing day matters got worse. The final blow came when God showed an outright preference for Abel's offerings over Cain's. This was too much for Cain's ego. He devised a plot to do away with Abel.

One day in the field, with stone in hand, Cain moved in for the kill. With a single, life-crushing blow, Cain set a precedent for all future Sharks.

Do you recognize the key characteristics of the Shark? Like Cain, every Shark wants his own way. Introduce another creature, such as a spouse, into the tank and look out!

In a marriage the Shark is the mate who can't stand to be bested. The thought of being criticized or told what to do likewise makes the Shark's blood boil. The Shark demands that he or she be the supreme, unchallenged ruler of the relationship. Any apparent questioning of this authority is quickly squelched. And like Abel's blood cried out from the ground, the voices of the Shark's victims cry out from households all over the world.

While Skunks are predominantly women, Sharks tend to be men. Just as we saw the roots of Skunkism in God's original judgment on the sin of mankind, so also we glimpse here insight on Sharkism. God had said to Eve:

> "Yet your desire shall be for your husband,
> *And he shall rule over you.*"

It was as if He were warning Eve of the Shark to come. For nothing appeals more to a Shark than rulership. He loves to rule. But the Shark's rulership is destructive and malevolent. He chews up anything that gets in his way.

Can you see how a Skunk and a Shark would kill each other in a marriage? The Skunk is busy trying to get her needs met, (though she is trying in all the wrong ways), and the Shark is caught up in trying to preserve a grotesque dictatorship that was never meant to be. Provocation and retaliation. Tit for tat. *Quid pro quo.* Neither willing to learn another way.

Why does the Shark act as he does? As with the Skunk, the Shark's behavior is both innate and learned. I have found that quite often the Shark's anger is born out of some deep, personal hurt that he has experienced. Because this hurt is never brought out into the open where it can be healed, it remains inside and festers until it finally breaks out in the form of a desire to hurt others.

## *Michael*

Michael was a Shark who was a victim of another's violence. I met him when he came—against his will—for counseling. Because of his abusiveness, he had been required by social service authorities to visit a counselor for a series of ten weekly sessions, or else risk being evicted from his home and losing access to his wife and children.

When he arrived for our first appointment, I was at the door to greet him as he came down the hall toward my office. But he ignored my outstretched hand and walked right on in. When I turned around I was surprised to find him sitting in my chair, the one I have positioned just a few feet from the couch where those who are being counseled normally sit. I casually took a seat on the couch. Without a doubt, Michael—whom I noticed was dressed to the hilt—preferred to be in charge.

"I want you to know that I am not here by my own choice," he began.

I knew that already. I opened my mouth to respond to him, but before I could say a word Michael rose from the chair and walked out of the room. He had succeeded in both beginning and ending our conversation with one sentence.

Our ten sessions were definitely off to a bad start.

Surprisingly, Michael kept returning week after week, and each time he stayed a little longer. I knew that legally he was required to attend these appointments, but as we continued to meet I sensed that he was motivated to come by more than just coercion. He recognized that I accepted him, and I think something inside him told him I was keenly aware of the hurt lying below the surface of his anger.

Soon Michael let me have a glimpse of that hurt, and as the weeks went by he opened up more and more—speaking often in tears—about the true source of his anger.

Michael's uncle had been quietly suspected of sexually abusing his nephews and nieces for years, but nobody ever followed up on the suspicions because of the man's prominent position in his community and church. Relatives could not or would not bring themselves to believe this man would do such a thing.

But Michael could believe it. He was one of the victims. He hated this man for the humiliating things his uncle had forced him to do. But, strangely, he hated his parents even more for not exposing and ending the abuse. Most of all, he despised himself for not being strong enough to have stopped it.

To make matters worse, the uncle had died a few years back. Now Michael felt as if he was left all alone with the knowledge of a horrible secret and no hope for revenge. Michael's beautiful wife and two little daughters then became the substitute target for his rage.

Now I could understand how Michael had become a Shark.

"I hate him! I hate him!" Michael sobbed. "I never *once* hated my wife and kids. It was *him. HIM!*"

Ever since his nightmare experience with his uncle, Michael had vowed never again to be dominated by anyone. He would make others pay for the hell he had been forced to experience. He would be the undisputed ruler, whatever the cost. In this case, the high cost of Michael's rulership was paid by his wife and children.

I wish I could say Michael is living a happier life now, but I can't. Unable to forgive his uncle, his parents, or himself, Michael abruptly ended his visits with me and chose to leave his family for a life of singleness in another city. I grieve for Michael and for the many others like him who have become Sharks for similar reasons. I grieve as well for their spouses and the children, who must live under their tyranny. Many of these little ones will grow up with the same burning anger Michael had; and like Michael, they will unleash it on those closest to them.

Are you a Shark? Do you hunger for rulership? Do those around you pay a painfully high price in their relationship with you? Perhaps you are a Shark because you have been badly hurt at some time in your life, or maybe you are one for no other reason than your sinful nature. Either way, you can find help for forgiving the past hurts and for learning a new way of relating to those whom you love. The final section in this book will outline that help.

## For Those Who Can't Relate

Perhaps you have not been able to identify in the least with either the Skunk or the Shark. You say sincerely to yourself, "I really don't fight like that. I don't nag and I certainly don't attack viciously. In fact, I don't fight at all."

Bingo! You are right! With all your might you seek to avoid conflict. Fight or flight is never a hard choice for you. You always choose the latter.

But did you know that by avoiding a fight you are often participating in one? Avoidance sometimes packs a mean punch. Ever wonder why psychologists call it "passive *aggression*"?

I can honestly say that I find it much easier to counsel a Skunk or a Shark than I do a Turtle. At least Skunks and Sharks put their feelings out in the open where we can work with them. But the Turtle's feelings are usually hidden.

If you think you might be one of these armored creatures, poke your head out of your shell long enough to read the next chapter.

# 21

# Hide and Seek

FEW ANIMALS have natural protection as excellent as that of the turtle, which is the world's only reptile with a shell. And of the 240 species of turtles, not a one of them has a vocal cord. The turtle has no true voice.

Spouses can be like turtles, too. The spouse who fights like a turtle frequently retreats inside his or her shell in an attempt to avoid a conflict. And like his namesake, the Turtle in a marriage seems also to have no true voice. The Turtle equates voicing one's opinion with open conflict, and the Turtle doesn't like open conflict.

Consequently we find the Turtle expressing his opinion in subtle, passive-aggressive ways. When the Turtle pouts or gives the cold shoulder treatment, he or she is really saying, "I don't like the way things are going here," or, "I'm hurting, and I want something to change."

But will the Turtle actually say these things? No way! That might start a conflict! But does the Turtle's spouse ever accurately interpret what the Turtle is trying to communicate? Only rarely! In fact, the message the Turtle conveys is usually far worse than it was intended to be.

Sometimes, though, the Turtle intentionally uses his silence to send some extremely cruel messages. Silence, in my opinion, is far worse than the sharpest of barbs. Silence says, "I reject you by shutting you out." Have you ever tried to resolve a conflict with someone who has totally shut you out?  As Simon and Garfunkel said in their classic song, *The Sounds of Silence:*

> "Fool!" said I, "You do not know.
> Silence like a cancer grows."

How similar to a malignant cancer is silence—the most devastating of the Turtle's tactics.  Homes in every city are riddled with this hushed disease.

If you are a Turtle, after reading this chapter you should find it hard to ever say again that you "never fight."  The truth is, you fight frequently—with your passive-aggressiveness and your silent treatment of others.  In fact, you are among the very worst of fighters!

I know...because I am a Turtle.  Here's a bit of my story.

## *Two Turtles in Paradise*

With the staccato screech of rubber on asphalt, the enormous 747 touched down, sped along the runway, and came to a halt.  Cindy, my bride of less than twenty-four hours, gave me an excited glance.  Both our hearts raced with anticipation.

The flight over from Kansas City had seemed endless, but we had finally arrived.  Our attendant swung open the door of the plane, and instantly a floral fragrance wafted through the cabin.  Over the intercom the pilot announced, "Welcome to colorful Maui.  Enjoy!"

We could not have hoped for a better honeymoon spot.  Our hotel was everything the brochures had pictured.  Gorgeous, fresh fruit was delivered every day to our room, which was the size of a small house.  Our bedspreads were turned down for us each night and the pillows adorned with a chocolate or an orchid.  There were waves to be played in, coves to be snorkeled in, and seafood galore to delight in. If we could stay here for the rest of our lives everything would be perfect—or so we thought.

Until this point in our relationship we had never had a fight. Looking back, I can see that all of the emotions for a potential conflict had been present during our

*the turtle*

courtship and engagement, but we had never chose to show them. We became skilled at retreating into our shells before things got heated. For Cindy, it so happens, is also a Turtle. There we were, honeymooning together in Hawaii—two married Turtles who were soon to find out why such a combination is potentially a dangerous one.

On the last day of our week-long stay on Maui, an incident occurred that sent us both into our shells. The weather during our trip had been depressing, and so was the thought of returning to the mainland with our bodies a lighter shade than when we left. As we were preparing to check out of the hotel, the sun finally made an appearance. "Let's stay longer," Cindy suggested. "I'm sure they'll give us an extension on our room."

The thought had crossed my mind, but I was sure that staying was not worth the hassle of unpacking. So, in dogmatic tones I stated, "Hotels like this fill up months in advance, Honey. I'm positive our room has already been given to someone else." Cindy agreed, but I could tell she was sorry to go home without a tan.

We loaded our luggage into our rental car and then returned to settle our account at the desk. While paying, I decided to verify my decision to leave. "Excuse me, sir," I said, "I think I already know the answer to this, but would it have been possible for us to have received a room extension?" His answer landed like an uppercut. "A room extension? Of course you can have one," he told us. But our bags were packed. It was too late.

Suddenly two happy honeymooners were transformed into sulking, silent Turtles. Cindy was upset. I was embarrassed. We both got quiet. Neither of us had ever seen the other act quite like this before. I remember taking the scenic drive to Hana that afternoon and not saying a word to each other the entire way. Here we were driving past some of the most beautiful scenery in Hawaii, unable to enjoy it. Instead, all we could feel was panic, rejection, and doubt over whether we should have ever married each other. My gut ached as I thought of living in silence for the rest of our lives. *What happened to the happy people we were just a few short hours ago?* I thought to myself. I'm sure Cindy had similar thoughts and feelings. But we did not know how to have an open conflict with each other.

Fortunately, we made it through that day with a desire to still be married. We have friends who, from time to time, recall their own honeymoons and speak of them as if they were the greatest experiences of all times. We grin sheepishly at each other because we can't truthfully say the same for ours. But our honeymoon did teach us something: We were made painfully aware that we are Turtles and that we needed to learn a different style of conflict.

Since then, both Cindy and I have learned enough that I can now refer to us as reformed Turtles. How about you? Are you a Turtle that needs reforming?

## *The Roots of Turtleism*

If we removed the shell of the average Turtle, underneath that hard exterior we would find one thing: *fear!* Herein lies the roots of Turtleism.

Have you ever been deathly afraid of something? What did you do? Did you run right up to the object of your fear and confront it? Or, did you cower in the shadows, hoping you would go unnoticed? If you're like most of us, you probably did the latter.

Adam and Eve did exactly the same thing. As soon as they disobeyed God, they were in a heap of trouble

and they knew it. They were afraid of God, so they hid
from Him. Here's the Bible's account of the story:

> The serpent was the craftiest of all the
> creatures the Lord God had made. So the ser-
> pent came to the woman. "Really?" he asked.
> "None of the fruit in the garden? God says you
> mustn't eat *any* of it?"
>
> "Of course we may eat it," the woman told
> him. "It's only the fruit from the tree at the cen-
> ter of the garden that we are not to eat. God
> says we mustn't eat it or even touch it, or we
> will die."
>
> "That's a lie!" the serpent hissed. "You'll
> not die! God knows very well that the instant
> you eat it you will become like him, for your
> eyes will be opened...you will be able to distin-
> guish good from evil!"
>
> The woman was convinced. How lovely
> and fresh looking it was! And it would make
> her so wise! So she ate some of the fruit and
> gave some to her husband, and he ate it too.
> And as they ate it, suddenly they became aware
> of their nakedness, and were embarrassed. So
> they strung fig leaves together to cover them-
> selves around the hips.
>
> That evening they heard the sound of the
> Lord God walking in the garden; and they hid
> themselves among the trees. The Lord God
> called to Adam, "Why are you hiding?"
>
> And Adam replied, "I heard you coming
> and didn't want you to see me naked. So I hid."
> (Genesis 3:1-10)

That's a pretty pathetic sight, isn't it? The man and
the woman, who had been made by God to be naked and
fully disclosed, were suddenly ashamed and afraid of
being known. When conflict arose, the royal couple of

the garden exchanged their crowns for the shell of a turtle.

If they could have had their "druthers," they would have hidden from God for the rest of eternity rather than admit to Him their disobedience. But that was never the way God intended it to be. I have a hunch that, before their sin, even conflict would have been a very normal part of God's scheme of things. After all, before Eve's arrival, there was never any need for Adam to hide the fact that he was discontent over being the only one of God's creation without a mate. Adam had full access to God; he could lay any request before Him. The garden was an open forum for all manner of topics to be discussed. If any one of God's handicraft had a beef, they could air it out with Him. So perhaps he came to God with his complaint and God complied.

Conflicting opinions were not taboo in God's new world. And I am sure that, had they possessed more foresight, Adam and Eve would have brought even their dilemma over the Tree of Knowledge to the Creator, and He would have fielded all their questions. That was not the case, though. Their disobedience led to conflict, which led to their fear of being known, which led to Turtleism. The pattern was established and it still exists today.

This fear of being known in marriage seems to arise especially in the two arenas in which we are most revealed and vulnerable—*sexual intimacy* and *conflict*. In this chapter, I will deal only with the fear of being known in conflict, but for those of you who may struggle with the fear of being known intimately in sex, I suggest that you read *The Gift of Sex* by Clifford and Joyce Penner.

Look back at Cindy's and my honeymoon. Fear caused us both to retreat. We were afraid our one-week-old marriage was already failing. Since our definition of a happy marriage at that time did not allow for an errant husband or disharmony in decision-making, I was afraid to admit my mistake, and Cindy was afraid to confront me.

## *Lollipops and Roses*

Think back with me to the days of your courtship. Most couples experience a time in their relationship where everything seems like lollipops and roses. This can be the happiest time of a couple's life together. It provides a treasure chest of memories they can enjoy for a long time.

But the dating and engagement periods are almost always characterized by showing off our strengths and hiding all our weaknesses. This is the "best-foot-forward-be-on-your-guard-never-let-em-see-you-sweat" segment in a relationship. We fear that if we were to ever share our true opinions on a matter, we might be rejected. If the girl likes something, you can be sure that the boy will like it, too, and vice versa.

Communication during this period goes something like this:

> *Boy:* You mean, you like browsing for entire days at busy, fashionable shopping malls with not even the remotest idea of what you are looking for? That's one of my favorite things, too!

> *Girl:* Championship wrestling?! I *love* championship wrestling! There's nothing I like better than to watch big, sweaty men pulverize each other while crazed fans scream foul language at the top of their lungs.

It may be normal communication for pre-married couples—but it isn't very honest. Sadly, many people carry this type of communication right on into marriage. When the honeymoon is over and the normal conflicts of marriage begin, some couples are grossly unprepared and unskilled at expressing themselves and getting their needs met. So, what do they do? They go into their shells and stew over the latest incompatibility between themselves and their mate. They become the "married singles" of our society. They are lonely and isolated despite their marital status. This is Turtleism at its worst. And in many ways it greatly overshadows the evils of the cruelest of Sharks.

Are you a Turtle? Then ask yourself, "What am I so afraid of?" Like most Turtles, you are probably afraid of anger and its potential effects. Whether it's your own or your opponent's anger makes no difference. Your assumption is that anger is a negative emotion, and that it is always destructive. Perhaps you had a Skunk and a Shark for parents, and you sincerely believe that your way is better than theirs. But you are kidding yourself. Remember: "Silence like a cancer grows."

If you are a Turtle, coming out of your shell requires you to do two things:

1. Drop the assumption that "happy marriages" are void of conflict.

2. Learn to fight using the rules presented in this book.

I invite you to join Cindy and me—two reformed Turtles—in the process of learning to fight right. We love who we are becoming. And frankly, the air is so much nicer outside those old, musty veneers we used to carry around with us.

If you aren't a Turtle, but your spouse is—then please be patient as he or she changes. After all...we Turtles are notoriously slow.

# 22

# The Name of the Game Is Blame

A MASTER OF DISGUISE—that's the chameleon. From green to red to orange to brown, this colorful lizard alters itself for protection. Without its ability to change, the chameleon is vulnerable to the attacks of numerous enemies. Often gracing the covers of wildlife magazines, these enigmas are surrounded by an air of mystery.

But Chameleons are also at home in the busiest of cities. Comfortable in a three-piece suit or jeans, they may be seen driving to work in a BMW or chauffeuring a vanload of kids to the park. Chameleons do, however, have one very important thing in common: They all respond to conflict the same way. They avoid fighting by distorting the facts.

## *Putting on the Mask*

"It wasn't *my* fault! How can you overlook the fact that you did the very same thing last week? I was merely following suit."

"Yes, I know I'm late for dinner, but I wouldn't be late if my client hadn't talked my ear off."

"Okay. So I drink a little, now and then. But I probably wouldn't if you didn't nag me so much."

On and on goes the Chameleon, excusing himself by blaming others, putting on the mask of innocence, distorting the facts of his own misdeeds.

Blame is the Chameleon's chief disguise. Do you use it frequently? If so, you are probably a Chameleon in your conflict style. You'll probably discover also that the rules violation you are most often guilty of is that of using "You" statements instead of "I" statements.

## *Bluffing in the Buff*

Once more, travel back with me to the book of Genesis and look again at the original conflict. When God questioned Adam and Eve about their disobedience, they each blamed someone else. And the buck has not stopped since. Here lies the roots of Chameleonism. Listen to the dialogue.

> *God:* "Adam, have you eaten from the tree of which I commanded you not to eat?"
> *Adam:* "Well, uh...you see, God...the woman you put here with me gave me the fruit, and I ate it."
> *God:* "Why did you do this, Eve?"
> *Eve:* "The snake tricked me into eating it."

The scene is almost comical, isn't it? Here are two naked people trying to bluff their way to an acquittal while standing before an all-knowing God. I can almost see the fingers pointing. "She did it!" "No, he did it!" "No, the snake did it—yeah, that's it! The snake did it." But God was not fooled.

Two simple and reliable tests can help you know whether you are a Chameleon. The first is to listen to the words you speak in a conflict to discover if your general tendency is to never use the pronoun "I." Instead you hear yourself saying, "*He* did it, too!" or, "*She* said it first!" or, "*You're* just as guilty!" If this is true for you, chances are you are a Chameleon.

The second test is also a gauge of the words you use in conflict. If you frequently qualify your statements with the word, "but," that's further evidence that you are a Chameleon. You say, "I can understand your point, *but...*" or, "I'm sorry I hurt you, *but...*" Note Adam's message to God: "Yes, I ate the apple, *but...* I wouldn't have if Eve hadn't tempted me. And besides, it's your fault for giving her to me in the first place." The Chameleon will blame anyone or anything...even to the point of blaming God.

## *The Turning Point*

When I counsel with a couple, it's for an average of eight to twelve weeks. Along the way, there is usually a turning point when suddenly everyone in the room recognizes that progress is being made. There is a feeling of heaviness lifted. Smiles restake their claim on facial wasteland. Fingers intertwine rather than indict one another. Blame has breathed its last.

For the first time, the couple has shaken off those weighty words like "but"..."still"..."yet"..."however." And a new word has been added to their vocabularies. That word is *I.*

"*I* was wrong."
"*I* can see how I hurt you."
"*I* understand."

If you're a Chameleon, there may be only one color you can turn at this moment—bright red. Like our friends in the garden, you have been caught with a mouthful of fruit.

Perhaps the best thing you can do now is admit the truth.

Go ahead. Say the words:


"My name is _____ ,

                          and I'm a **Chameleon!**"

# part iv

# The Master
of Conflict

# 23

# Doing Battle with God

ACCORDING TO HISTORIANS, since 3500 B.C. the earth has experienced only 292 years without any type of warfare.   We are, you might say, a planet in love with conflicts.

We've had some doozers—the World Wars of this century come automatically to mind, while history buffs will know about such sweeping conflicts as the Hundred Years' War, the Thirty Years' War, the Wars of the Roses, the Gallic Wars, the Punic Wars, and a long list of wrenching revolutions and civil wars.

But if you're impressed with the dread and drama of these, you haven't seen anything until you have read through the Bible.  It is the account par excellence of revolution...and resolution.

Creation at war with its Creator!  Can you imagine it? Man shaking his fist at Heaven, demanding his rights from the Divine—and at the heart of the matter, man seeking to take over the very throne of God.

It adds up to a rather poor battle strategy.  The odds aren't much in our favor, are they?  Mankind doing battle with God is like Rhode Island challenging the United States to a civil war—not a wise decision.

If you were God, would you tolerate rebellion from

your creation? Would you bend over backwards to reach some sort of compromise with them? Would you ignore them and hope that everything sort of ironed itself out? Would you plead with them and beg them to accept your authority? Or would you divorce yourself from them and start all over again with another planet?

Fortunately for us, God didn't do any of the above.

*doing battle with God*

In fact, not in a million years could we have formulated God's plan of conflict resolution.

The Cross explains it all.

## Dying to Resolve

*The Cross*...God's ultimate plan of conflict resolution...The death of His Son on a human meat-rack. This was God's method of putting an end to the war between Himself and His creation. How amazing is the Cross, and yet, how offensive it is to most of us. In the Bible, both Paul and Peter indicate that the Cross is the central historical fact that men and women will stumble over and be offended by throughout the ages. And why is the Cross so offensive to humanity? One reason is that we are so skeptical of anything that is free. To us an advertisement that says, "Free" means that there may well be something wrong with the product, or that it's of little value anyway. Therefore, we reason, the free gift of salvation offered by the Cross cannot be worth much. We are a people used to freedom costing something. We gain our salvation the old-fashioned way: We *earn* it!

Perhaps what offends us most about the Cross is that if we finally take it seriously, it will require us to change the ways we handle our conflicts with God and with other people. We can no longer view God as an angry ogre in the sky who deserves to be fought with. We can no longer hate our parents for all the ways they ruined our childhood. We can no longer blame our spouse or our children for robbing us of freedom and happiness.

In fact, the Bible tells us we must develop an entirely new attitude. Paul says in Philippians 2: 5-8—

> Your attitude should be the kind that was shown us by Jesus Christ, who, though he was

> God, did not demand and cling to his rights as
> God, but laid aside his mighty power and glory,
> taking the disguise of a slave and becoming like
> men.  And he humbled himself even further,
> going so far as actually to die a criminal's death
> on a cross.

Are you clinging to your rights as "husband" or
"wife" or "parent" or "rebellious teenager"?  When you
have been wronged by a family member, do you feel the
offender should pay for his or her mistakes?

If so, consider this.  If anyone deserves to cling to his
rights, it is God.  It was He who created a perfect world
and placed us in it.  It was we who proceeded to mess up
that perfect world.  In His anger God could have annihi-
lated the whole ball of wax and gone about His business
elsewhere, but He didn't.  Instead, God forgave us by
taking our punishment on the Cross.

What a strange thing forgiveness is!  The acceptance
of it can cause a man to turn around and, almost without
thought, extend mercy to the most hideous of criminals.
The rejection of it can cause a man to inflict sadistic tor-
ture upon the meekest of human beings.  It was this rejection of forgiveness that caused the man in Matthew 18,
who had been pardoned of a ten-million-dollar debt, to
seek out the man who owed him two-thousand dollars
and try to choke it out of him.  It was this rejection of forgiveness that caused the Pharisees in Jesus' days to plot
and carry out His death during Passover week.  It is this
same rejection of forgiveness that causes people like you
and me to engage in destructive conflict with our families.  The Bible indicates that when we accept that we
have been forgiven much, only then can we love much.
Only then can our families experience constructive conflict.  How much have you been forgiven?  How much
are you in the habit of forgiving others?

Before you begin to truly understand the rules of conflict, you must develop the following attitude about yourself and the person with whom you are in conflict:

> *As one who has been forgiven so much by God,*
> *I have no right to consider my opponent as anything less*
> *than an object of my forgiveness.*
> *If I have wronged my opponent,*
> *then I owe him nothing short of an apology.*

Let me ask you again: Do you want better conflict resolution in your family? If you do, you must realize that all the rules in all the conflict resolution books in the world cannot bring peace to your home. Try as you may to "fight right" with your loved ones, eventually you will run out of steam. You may master every conflict rule in this book, but if you do not know the Master of conflict, you will continue to hurt one another. God's Son died to resolve the war between creation and Creator. And He is dying for us to do likewise with one another.

## Fact and Feeling

All this talk of forgiveness may have raised a few questions for you: "Is the absence of anger a prerequisite for me to forgive my spouse?" "If I am mad at my children, does that mean that I haven't forgiven them?" "Is the presence of anger a contradiction of forgiveness?" The answer to all three is "No!"

The expression of anger towards one with whom we are conflicting is no more a contradiction of forgiveness than is the surgeon's incision a contradiction of his desire to heal his patient of cancer. The greater sin occurs when the surgeon refuses to make the incision and the cancer grows until it kills the patient.

The same thing happens when we refuse to express our anger with one another. Cancer eats away at both the relationship and the person in whom the anger remains. This is how the Turtle handles his anger. He stuffs it all inside his shell until finally he is overwhelmed by depression, or else he explodes when the pressure becomes too great. The Bible seems to disagree specifically with this method of handling anger.

"Be angry," the Bible says, "and yet do not sin." Shocking, isn't it! God actually commands us to be angry. I can't tell you how many times I have referred to this verse with people in counseling. Their responses are almost always ones of disbelief. "You're crazy! Let me see that Bible!" said one young man with whom I had just shared this revelation. "Wow! I guess it's true," he concluded. I am amazed at the number of people, especially Christians, who have adopted the notion that anger and forgiveness are mutually exclusive, or that anger and conflict resolution cannot coexist. That would be like saying that a feeling and a fact could not both be true at the same time. And yet, everyday we make decisions that involve both fact and feeling, simultaneously.

An example: Little Bobby must have his breakfast by 7:30 A.M. or he will miss his school bus. So you set your alarm for 6:45 in order to accommodate him. You don't deny the fact that your son's need is legitimate. But that doesn't stop you from being generally crabby and cursing the toaster. You see, our actions are governed both by fact and feeling. Rarely can the two be separated. They are constant partners.

This is equally true of anger and forgiveness—one a feeling, the other a fact. The title of Gary Smalley's excellent marriage seminar is "Love Is a Decision." I am certain he would agree with me that the equation applies also to forgiveness. Forgiveness is a decision—a decision based on facts. It has nothing whatsoever to do with feelings. Let me illustrate.

FACT: My son has just backed the family station wagon into the garbage cans.

FACT: If I've told him once, I've told him forty-seven times to watch where he is going—especially when he is driving the car in reverse.

FACT: I do not have the cash to buy another set of garbage cans, let alone a new paint job for the car.

FACT: However, my son's offense, compared to the countless times I have offended and disobeyed God, is quite small. If God can forgive me, surely I can forgive my son.

Based on the facts, I choose to forgive my son. That doesn't mean I have no feeling about my son's obvious negligence. In fact, I am quite furious with him. I am so mad that if I don't stop and consider the facts above, especially the fourth one, I am liable to be very destructive in my approach with him. Forgiving my son also doesn't mean that I will not apply some measure of discipline to my son. I will probably restrict his use of the car until he can pay for the cans and the paint job. All I am saying is that, based on the facts, I have decided to forgive my son.

Now, you may be thinking, "Okay. I can buy the fact that you have forgiven your son based on the facts. But what good does that do your son? After all, he still has to pay for the damage." Yes, but my attitude of forgive-

ness does him a lot of good.  It is this attitude that prevents me from breaking all the rules of conflict we have
discussed in this book.  Because I have chosen to forgive
my son based on the facts, I commit myself to not yell at
him, or demean him, or provoke him to anger with my
harshness.  It is my attitude of forgiveness that gives my
son the sense of acceptance from me that says,  "I am
angry with you for backing the car into the garbage cans,
but I still accept you because, frankly, you are worth
more to me than a million garbage cans."

## More than the Stars and the Birds

True forgiveness is never *based* on feelings.  I am
quite certain that Jesus did not feel like forgiving us
while He hung on the cross.  It is very possible that He
was angry at the mob as they jeered at Him and spat
upon Him.  Nevertheless, He considered the facts and
made His decision to forgive.

FACT:  "All have sinned and fallen short of the glory
of God." (Romans 3:23)

FACT:  "The wages of sin are death." (Romans 6:23)

FACT:  "I am the Way, the Truth, and the Life.  No
man comes to the Father, but by me." (John 14:6)

Because of these facts, Jesus had mercy on us and
chose to forgive us, though I am sure that it was not
without feeling that He made His decision.

The entire message of this book hinges upon this one
fact: *Only when we have allowed God to establish residence
in our hearts, do we hold the key to having a good family*

*fight.* The other things written between these covers are merely helpful rules and guidelines.

In spite of all our sins, God still holds us in high esteem. He says that we are more valuable to Him than all the stars in the sky and more precious than all the birds of the air—and yes, worth more than even a million garbage cans. The next time you are about to conflict with someone in your family, stop and ask yourself these questions:

> "How much has God forgiven me?"
> "How much worth has He assigned me?"

Then, turn toward your opponent and offer the same forgiveness, and the same assessment of worth.

## *The Governor's Rules*

History is like a giant negotiation table with God sitting on one side and humanity on the other. God's every offer has been calculated, culminating in His final offer—the handing over of His Son to death. I believe that God had a plan all along concerning how He would win sinful humanity back to Himself. He established some rules of conflict resolution and He stuck to them. After all, God is the Governor who invented the rules and gave them to us.

Today you are living in Adams Crossing. It can be a cold and lonely place, can't it? Spouses and families generally aren't as happy as they were intended to be back in New Woods Ferry. Fortunately, God has left us a book that shows us how to get along with each other. It is the Governor's book, and we call it the Bible.

Reach into the gift of pain again. There at the bottom of the package you will find one last box. Open it. Inside is a copy of this magnificent book. In it, God demonstrates, by living example, how we can follow the rules of a good fight. The following chapters are taken right out of the Bible and designed to parallel the rules you read about in section two. I urge you to become familiar with the Bible. Find out how God resolves conflicts; for in doing so, your conflicts with one another will become more manageable. You and your family will no longer be fighting alone. You'll be going to battle...with God at your side.

# 24

# The World's Longest Fuse

I'VE BUILT SAND CASTLES many times, but never anything like the one constructed in April 1986 on Treasure Island, Florida. Standing five stories high ( 52.8 feet, to be exact) and weighing 48,000 tons, the "Lost City of Atlantis" was the tallest and perhaps largest sand structure ever built.

I also have juggled balls, eaten pancakes, flown a kite, and kissed a woman...but I hold no records in these events either. Three balls and three pancakes are about all I can manage at one time, which are nothing compared to the exploits of Albert Lucas and Peter Dowdeswell. Lucas once juggled seven balls for more than two minutes. Dowdeswell, world champion glutton, downed sixty-two pancakes in less than seven minutes.

As for kissing and kite flying, the real virtuosos are Eddie Levin and Delphine Cray of Chicago, and Harry N. Osborne. Osborne holds the record for the longest recorded flight of 180 hours and seventeen minutes, while Eddie and Delphine once kissed for seventeen days. You may be more interested to know that the longest cinematic kiss goes to Regis Toomey and Jane Wyman (the first Mrs. Ronald Reagan) when they held it for 185 seconds in *You're In the Army Now*.

*The Guinness Book of World Records* lists these and an amazing array of other accomplishments and stunts—some daring, some wacky, some downright awe-inspiring. But one record omitted by the book deserves mention: The person with the world's longest fuse.

## Let My People Go!

Recently, a king came to Denver. He didn't make his entrance in the royal manner one expects from a king. Instead, he rode boxed-up and banded tightly on the back of a truck. The newspapers heralded his arrival:

### RAMESES II COMES TO TOWN!

With assistance from burly crewmen, the king disembarked and established residence in the Queen City, which he was to call home for the next nine months. He brought with him crate after crate of his belongings, the contents of which many fine citizens flock to pay their homage—and their hard-earned currency.

I have yet to see this famous exhibit. But I have some previous knowledge about this Rameses fellow. He is—I should say *was*—the ruler of a vast Egyptian empire. Many historians believe him to be the pharaoh of the Exodus. He was the keystone of his society, blessed with extraordinary wealth, and revered as the intermediary between gods and men. Some even honored Rameses as a god himself. In terms of material goods, he had everything, including legions of Hebrew slaves to build his monuments of personal deification. Rameses II lacked no good thing—except, perhaps, common sense in doing business with the God of the Israelites.

"Let my people go!" commanded the Hebrew God.

"I'll do as I please!" replied Rameses.

In return for Rameses' arrogance, God laid His finger on the pulse of Egypt and squeezed tightly. With hordes of frogs, swarming lice, and flies, He choked the flow of life from the pharaoh's kingdom. Still, the stubborn ruler refused to grant the Hebrews' freedom. God persisted. He sent plagues upon the Egyptians' livestock and ghastly boils upon their bodies. But Rameses stood his ground. So God blighted the land with hailstones big enough to kill men, animals, trees, and crops. Rameses' advisors pleaded with their master to give in, but still he would not. Therefore, God blanketed the entire countryside with a thick layer of locusts and darkness, stripping the fields of greenery and the people of eyesight. And with a crack of doom, He cut short the life of every Egyptian firstborn—man *and* beast.

Finally, in anguish, Rameses cried, "Take them! Take all of them! Take your people and go!"

## The Tempered Temper

And so God led His people out of Egypt, and He gave them this reminder and promise: "I have rescued you from the drudgery and humiliation you were undergoing. Now I will lead you to a land flowing with milk and honey, and I will surely give this land to you."

What a promise! And what great pains God took to fulfill His promise. The people were barely beyond the city limits and already He had performed miracles that broke their shackles and baffled the court magicians. Here was God now in their midst, shading them by day as a great cloud and leading them by night as a pillar of fire.

When the angry Egyptians chased them in hopes of reclaiming their property, God opened wide the mouth of the Red Sea and the Israelites walked through on dry land.  But the pursuing army was swallowed whole.

When the Israelites became hungry, God showered them with bread and birds to eat.  And when their throats were parched, He quenched their thirsts by causing water to flow from the rocks of the desert.

But in spite of God's faithfulness, the people grumbled against Him.  It was only a matter of days before they had forgotten His graciousness.  And after a few weeks' journey from Egypt, they were dancing before other deities.

God's fuse was lit!

So angry was God at these infidels that the Bible says He wanted to wipe them all out.  How dare they make a mockery of His miraculous mercy.  But Moses pleaded with God to withhold His wrath, and fortunately for the Hebrews, God complied.  He tempered His temper.  And for forty years He put up with their whining and complaining until finally He brought them into the promised land.

A forty-year fuse!  Can you imagine holding your temper for that long?  Actually, the Bible indicates that God's fuse was lit long before this incident.  Since the inauguration of the world, God's anger has raged against His disobedient creation.  But even after we murdered His Son on a cross, thousands, perhaps millions of years later, His fuse still burns brightly...because He loves us and desires that we all should enter into friendship with Him before His fuse comes to an end.

## The Wilderness of Wedlock

If you are married, then you have made a promise

too. At the altar you assured your spouse of your undying love. Like God to the Israelites, you made a vow to walk with your partner through the wilderness of wedlock. In light of your promise, consider the self-control it took for God to refrain from crushing the idolatrous Israelites after all He had done for them. Maybe your patience has been tried periodically during your own

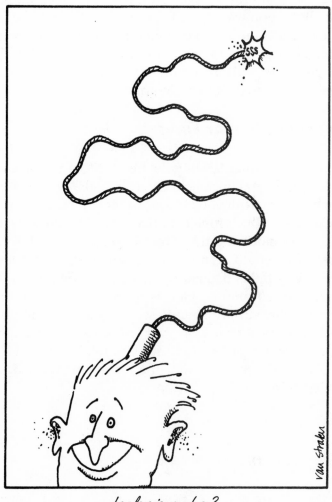

*how long is your fuse?*

marriage journey. Perhaps you, too, on occasion have bankrupted yourself for your spouse or your children, and received a cold slap in return. God knows exactly how you are feeling. And He wants to help you respond positively.

Remember that there is a right and wrong time to fight. It is the untempered temper that violates Off-sides—the unbridled explosion that crushes the loved one. But if you want to fulfill your promise of "till death do us part," you must be willing to pull back the reigns of anger from time to time. If you do, your trek through married life will resemble an oasis rather than a continuous stretch of fiery desert.

## *How Long Is Your Fuse?*

What is it that lights your fuse? More importantly, how long do you burn before you explode? The fact that you get angry with your spouse or other family members is expected. But problems arise when the distance between the match and the bomb is microscopic. In reality, most of us could stand to have our fuses lengthened. Fair family fights depend upon what the Bible calls *patience* and *self-control*. God is the source of both these virtues. His supply is endless, and out of it He gives freely to those who ask. If your temper is too often ignited, ask God for patience and self-control.

After all, He does hold the record for the world's longest fuse.

# 25

# God in the Backfield

## Real Estate Heir Cashes in Holdings, Departs His Family

In a move that startled observers, Sonny P. Rodigal, youngest son of land-rich F. P. Rodigal, announced yesterday the full liquidation of his shares in his father's real estate empire.

Rodigal made the announcement in a meeting with the press just hours before his intended departure to a destination he described only as "a distant land." He indicated the move was planned as a permanent one away from his family.

Rodigal is the second of two sons born to F. P. Rodigal, who built his fortune through extensive Mediterranean holdings.

The senior Rodigal could not be reached for comment.

Are you interested when you read such journalism? Would you bother to glance through it again? Probably not. In reality, the manic-depressive nature of today's stock market overshadows the trivial account of a brash upstart's break from his father's business. One is news, the other is wasted ink. But the Bible gives us the rest of Sonny's story. And it is worth a second look.

## The Prodigal Son

The Prodigal Son...I have heard the story a thousand times. Every preacher's files contain a sermon on it. And if you sat through all of them, no two would be identical. This is not to say the majority of clergymen practice editorial license when they handle the Word of God. It does demonstrate the numerous angles from which one might approach this famous story told by Jesus.

The story can be told from the viewpoint of each character: a father, and his two boys. My favorite version is when the tale is recounted through the eyes of the father. Come with me now to a rambling farm in the Mediterranean countryside. At the center of the estate is a mansion bordered on all sides by golden crops. Cattle graze in the distance. A few servants are hurrying to finish chores before the sun deserts them.

On the porch sits the farms owners, his eyes trained on the road that extends past his property and toward the ocean. He is a wounded father, watching for his wayward son. During the day, he pushes back his sorrow with hard work, but a closer look reveals that he has cried many tears.

His youngest had always been a rebel. Although it was no shock when his son asked for his inheritance and declared that he was leaving, it hurt when he let the boy go. Now the pain of worry broke him with every night-fall. But he would not cease his vigil until the prodigal returned. He could only hope and wait.

Months pass. A harvest comes, goes, and then comes again. Then one evening, as the sun casts its farewell shadows, a figure appears on the horizon. The father squints, trying to bring the distant speck into focus. In the past he had been prematurely excited only to discover that what he thought was his son was nothing more than a stray cow that had slipped through a hole in the fence. This time, though, the speck walks upright with limbs that swing instead of plod.

The speck draws nearer. The father squints. It draws nearer. The father stands. It draws nearer. The father leaps from the porch.

"It is him! It's *my son!*"

"He is home!"

## What Would You Do?

How does the father respond now that his son has come home? Does he stand in the front yard, tapping his foot, waiting for the runaway to apologize? Does he turn his back and walk into the house, refusing to talk to the boy until he has proven his allegiance again? Or does he seize the opportunity to tongue-lash his son for all the anguish he has caused the family? As you ponder the conclusion, consider what your own response would be. What would you do if you were the father?

Often when I am in conflict with someone who has hurt me, I violate the rules by digging up all my old hurts and presenting them in a neat package to my foe. "See what you have done to me? Look at all the ways you have caused me grief."

I then proceed through the list, stating my case, hopeful that my opponent will apologize and beg forgiveness. But this tactic never has worked, because this is Backfield in Motion. No one likes to be brought to trial for all of his past crimes.

If you were the Prodigal Son's father would you be tempted to engage in a little Backfield in Motion? Would you remind your boy of the emotional stress he caused you that first month he was gone? Would you bring out your financial ledger and show him how much he has depleted your net worth in the last two years? What would you do?

In Jesus' story, the father did none of the above. He never resorted to Backfield in Motion. Instead, he invited his son back into the family and reinstated him in a position of high honor. The Prodigal Son is actually a story of how God treats you and me.

## Welcome Home Child!

All of us have rebelled against God and walked away from Him at some time.

"I'd prefer to go it alone...to do it my way," we tell God.

His response is always to wait and hope that one day we might return to Him. Some of us choose to make that journey home; others do not. But if and when we do return to God, His arms are wide open to receive us:

*"Welcome home, child! I am glad you're back!"*

Today you might find yourself in conflict with a family member. It may seem as if they are so far away that you have to squint to see them clearly. But as your eyes focus, you realize that the one with whom you are fighting really *is* the same person to whom you said "I do" years ago, or the same child you cheered into the world.

Do yourself a favor. Get up from your chair, run across the field, and greet that person with a warm embrace.

And one more thing: Don't bring up the past.

# 26

# Businessman's Bible

IT'S HIGH TIME someone invented another Bible translation—and I have an idea for one.

Of course some people will oppose it. I'll probably be called a heretic. But at least I'll be in good company. King James himself was criticized for his work. So was Tyndale House Publishers in the 1960s, when they parted ways with the good king and gave us *The Living Bible*.

So, I propose to you the Bible of the 1990s, appropriately titled:

*GOD'S-WORD-AT-A-GLANCE*

This handsome Bible is the perfect gift for friends, associates, clients, or . . . yourself. Everyone can benefit from the use of *God's-Word-at-a-Glance*. Imagine this. Every parable, every allegory, every historical event plotted chronologically in thirty-minute segments. "What time of day did God create Adam?" "When did Jonah and the whale have lunch?" "How long did it take Jesus to preach the Sermon on the Mount?" It's all there, just for you!

And if you act now, you'll receive the handy *Pocket-Word-at-a-Glance*—free of charge! Each Bible is available in western coach leather, hampshire pigskin, bonded cowhide, or supported vinyl. Take your pick. It's *your* choice.

Hold it!

Stop the commercial!

I am kidding of course. But the idea has some merit. After all, the language of today IS "time and how to manage it." You can keep your "thee's" and "thou's". What we want is a Bible that speaks our dialect . . . one that gives us records, and scheduled events, and services rendered. And would someone please tell us how Jesus accomplished all that stuff in just three years?

## *The Master and Stress*

Modern man wants desperately to manage his stress. You and I are told that prayer is the answer, but sometimes we can't relate. We look at Jesus and the culture in which He lived, and what we see is life at a snail's pace. Surely Jesus had no worries, no real deadlines to meet, no appointments to keep.

But Jesus was no stranger to stress. In fact, the stress He faced was hardly different from that of the modern man or woman in business. There was corporate opposition daily from the Pharisees, and the headaches of managing His disciples. There were the expectations of the masses who placed Jesus in great demand and called for an emphasis on public relations. And like today's executive, His job often forced Him to travel many miles and work late into the night.

Moreover, Jesus' family also contributed to His stress. He had to cope with constant sibling rivalry with brothers who saw Him as a man, but refused to worship Him as Messiah. There was the probable death of His father, Joseph, when Jesus was a teenager, (although the Bible is silent on this). Yet, we read that He knew the secret of mastering stress:

> *Enjoy the present by leading a balanced life. Let today's troubles be enough for today, and don't worry about tomorrow.*

No one has ever been quite as "present-minded" as was Jesus. Who else could sleep peacefully in the middle of a squall at sea? Who else could calmly wash others' feet one evening, knowing that his own feet would be pierced by nails the following day? No one else but Jesus. He is the master of "the now". He alone holds the key to a stress-free life. But when and how did He learn all this? After all, the Bible mentions little of His life.

## The Balanced Life

True, on the topic of Jesus' teenage years, the Bible is a stingy informant. It's as if He finished elementary school and then vanished for nearly two decades. All we know of this time span is that Jesus obeyed His parents and that He "grew in wisdom, in stature, and in favor with God and man." But perhaps in light of what the Bible says about Jesus' final three years on earth, that is all you and I need to know.

When we finally catch up with Jesus again, He is a mature man of thirty. Confident, yet humble. Or-

ganized, yet spontaneous. He is a man going places...
not wanting to waste a step. Were we to steal a look at
His daily planner, we might see the following:

|  |  |
|---|---|
| 5:00 A.M.— | Up to meditate and study the Torah. (Don't forget special prayer requests for Peter.) |
| 6:30 A.M.— | Wake the boys. Breakfast (figs and bread). |
| 7:15 A.M.— | Walk to Capernaum (spend time with Thomas along the way.) |
| 4:30 P.M.— | Arrive in Capernaum. Eat. |
| 5:00 P.M.— | Public ministry (healing) until bedtime. |
| 12:30 A.M.— | Prayer. |
| 1:00 A.M.— | Sleep. |

If ever there was a busy man, it was Jesus. Talk about
an imbalance of supply and demand! The noise of the
crowds crying for His help would be enough to convince
the average human being to resign from the job of Messiah. But not so with Jesus. He seemed to have an inex-
haustible reservoir of energy. To discover its source, look
at what the Bible says about His teenage and young adult
years.

Picture a young man as he prepares to become the
Savior of the world, increasingly aware that his role as

God in the flesh will bring more pain than praise in his future. He knows cruel conflict lies ahead for him. Every temple visit reminds him of it. The smell of altar sacrifices . . . bloody and bleating . . . will not let him escape the thought. He will someday die a slow death, pinioned to a cross.

If you were in His sandals, how would you cope? What would you fill your life with to endure the stress of such a pending conflict? Here's what Jesus did:

> He grew in wisdom and stature, and in favor
> with God and man. (Luke 2:52)

In other words, Jesus did four things.

1. He expanded His mind daily, growing in wisdom by committing the Old Testament to memory and obeying it.

2. He nurtured His body, staying healthy by eating right, (often fasting), and exercising daily, (walking hundreds of miles in His lifetime.)

3. He spent time with God, the Father, in prayer and meditation.

4. He cultivated friendships with men and women.

The end result was a balanced man able to handle stress. Yes, He was divine. But in many ways He was just like you and me . . . subject to overload, and susceptible to burn out.

Ultimately, the time came for Jesus to drink the cup of conflict that had been poured for Him long before His stable birth. And where do we find Him? In a garden, doing what He had always done when faced with stress. There He is, kneeling against a rock, a few good friends close by. Like so many times before, He is talking to His Father. And if we could hear His thoughts, perhaps we would recognize words of the ancient prophets that He had studied since boyhood:

> He will be condemned as a criminal.

But as we continue listening closely we can hear Him say,

> Not *my* will, but *yours* be done.

Soon the mob comes to take Him away, and He goes quietly...confidently. Jesus was prepared for His garden. Are you prepared for yours?

## *Your Own Special Garden*

In your busy, life-at-a-glance-world, how do you spell stress? Is it coming home after a day's work to a houseful of maniacal children? Is it finally reaching the bottom of the pile of bills only to discover the "Honey-do" list? Whatever the case, I'm sure that you, just like Jesus, have your own special garden filled with stress and anxiety. You may not be facing crucifixion, but an irate boss or a demanding family may seem to you a close second. It is here in your garden that you come to the end of your rope . . . and stare blankly at a noose.

Look around you, though. The scenery in your garden is quite different than that of the Savior's. Unlike His, yours is void of friends. I'm not talking about paper-thin acquaintances. I mean the type of friend that would eat a piano if he could then sing you to sleep. This is the friend who will do anything to soothe your stress. But this type takes cultivation. And if you haven't done that, then your garden is a very lonely place indeed.

And why is it that stress always catches you on an empty stomach? Have you come to the garden under-fed? How then, my friend, will you ever bear your burdens?

And listen! There is silence in your garden, with no dialogue between Father and child, not even a thought about what He may be trying to tell you in His Word. You are all alone...hungry...friendless...Godless...reeling under the weight of stress.

## *The Unbalanced Life*

If I have described the landscape in your garden, then unfortunately you have set yourself up for some awful family fights. I have seen both men and women crumble under the pressure of the work place, and then take it all out on their families. They keep piling it on down at the office, and then wonder why they are so venomous when they come home. The problem is not that they work hard. After all, Jesus worked harder than an entire corporation of these people. The problem is lack of balance, with work far outweighing all else. God and golf, food and family, books and buddies...all have been bumped off the busy schedule. It is no wonder, then, that they are ill-prepared when it's time to go to the garden of stress.

Jesus, Himself, spent most of His life learning to stay out from under the pile. And when it came time for His enemies to load it on at Calvary, He didn't fold under the pressure. He had grown in wisdom and, therefore, was able to answer wisely the accusations brought against Him. He had grown in stature, and so could withstand the whip. He had grown in favor with God and man, and consequently continued to do so as He hung on the cross, talking to His Father and imparting new life to the thief at His side.

Unfortunately, many poor family fights are the result of what I have been talking about in this chapter: one-dimensional lives, void of wisdom, health, friends, and, most of all, God. Because we are unbalanced people, we are unable to handle our stress. Consequently, we are unprepared to participate fairly in a family fight. And it will take more than a Businessman's Bible to combat the problem. It will take a focused effort on our part to grow mentally, physically, socially, and spiritually.

But even after hard work, you may not notice an immediate change in the fights at home. Stress has taken its toll. And it takes almost as much time for a person to get unwound as it did for him to get wound up in the first place. But don't let the slowness of the process discourage you from getting started. You must begin preparing right away for your next garden appointment. Your family fights depend upon it.

Sooner than you think, the mob will come for you again. Another conflict will break out in your little band of loved ones, and you will be asked to participate. How will you respond?

With a healthy body? Or a haggard brow?
With a clear mind? Or a cluttered consciousness?
With a godly perspective? Or a godless panic?
With an enlivened spirit? Or a lonely soul?

# 27

# Making the Most of Our Bad Decisions

HAVE YOU EVER waited at a stoplight and wondered what do do to pass the time?  The next time you're traffic-bound, conduct a mini-study in sociology.  Watch the people as they walk by.  Pay extra attention to one group—junior-highers.

Yesterday, while driving to work, I saw every color known to man (and some unknown) as a group of junior high kids passed through the crosswalk in front of me.  There were fluorescent pink socks pulled tightly over faded jeans, followed by Michael Jackson coats, electric red and laden with twenty pounds of silver zippers.  And one boy wore the same shade at both ends, his hair and hightops a bright, nuclear yellow.  I caught a glance of his purple backpack—then the light turned green, and I pulled away feeling blue.

I drove for several blocks and vowed that no child of mine would ever leave the house looking like that.  Fortunately, I slowed my mental crusade long enough to hear myself.  Only then did I begin to recall how I had dressed in junior high.

## "In" and "Out"

When I attended Hoover Junior High, sailor jeans were "in" and belts were "out"...along with shirttails, which one wore out if he wanted to be "in." Gold chains could be worn in or out, because either way was "in." But hair above the ears labeled one weird, whether his clothes were "in" or "out".

Suddenly I remembered how confusing life was back then. And by the time I reached work, I realized that things have not changed much since I was thirteen. Kids still dress like color-blind Van Goghs. And parents still look bewildered as their young impressionists head for school each morning.

As I walked up the sidewalk to my office, briefcase in hand and slacks neatly pressed, I asked myself, *How did I ever make it through those years?*

## *Wonder of Wonders*

It's a wonder parents ever let their children make decisions for themselves. It's a greater wonder that you and I allow each other this privilege. After all, both of us think we'd make pretty fair candidates to run the universe if given the chance. Often the slightest proposal from the other makes our minds slip into veto mode. That's when we begin to goal tend. But God does not goal tend. For our sakes, He let's us decide.

An excellent way to understand God is to view Him as the parent of a rebellious eighth grader. That image alone gives us a wealth of insight into how God relates to humanity. He is like the father who tells his teen to wear a coat because the weather outside is subfreezing. None of the youngster's friends are wearing coats so he doesn't want to wear one either. He wants to fit in, to be cool.

And that's exactly what he is as he turns his face into the wind and trudges to school. Real cool. The parent aches, knowing that his child is unprepared to meet the cold.

If you have been in that parent's shoes before, you have faced the struggle between knowing what's best for your child, and not wanting to make the decision for him. Perhaps you have seen your child leave in the morning dressed like an alien from outer space, and with friends whom you preferred would return to their planet. You would gladly pay for their tickets. Nevertheless, you smile and wave out the window.

It is always hard for a parent to allow a child to begin making decisions for himself. The same could be said for the spousal relationship. Let's examine how God dealt with His defiant children—how He committed Himself to not violating the rule of goal tending. Perhaps you and I can learn a lesson.

## *The Not-So-Kingly Kings*

"We want a king and we won't take 'no' for an answer!" badgered bratty Israel. "We want a real king...one we can see...just like all the other countries have!"

God, the parent, thought for a moment. He knew it was not to their advantage to have a king. Kings had a knack for starting armies, which inevitably led to the draft. Mothers would lose their sons to war, or at best to the drudgery of forging weapons. Others would be forced, without pay, to harvest the royal crops. The daughters of Israel would become maids of the court. And the king would seize their best fields and vineyards and give them to his friends. Being ruled by a king was certainly not in Israel's favor. Nevertheless, God granted their wish. And soon all of the above came to pass.

Saul, the premier king, wasted no time at all. For his debut battle against the Ammonites, he enlisted 330,000 men who had no choice in the matter. It was either fight for the king, or be cleft in two.

In time, Saul was replaced by David, a man after God's own heart. But he also had a heart for women. Ultimately, David's lust was his downfall. Great opportunity was given to the enemies of the Lord to despise and blaspheme Him. Israel had become a laughingstock.

Later, David again disobeyed God by taking a census of the people in order that he might boast in his great power. His arrogance invited a God-appointed plague upon the nation. In just three days, 70,000 men were dead.

So far, the Israelites had known only two kings. Already they realized that the quest for political equality with their neighbors was not cost-effective. But more kings followed.

Solomon brought wealth and power to Israel. During his reign, silver was as common as stones in the city of Jerusalem. But like his father, Solomon was easily influenced by women. And he took for himself many foreign wives who led him into idolatry. The people followed their ruler's lead, and soon all of Israel bowed at the feet of strange deities. There they remained for three and a half centuries. Take a look at some of the kings that followed.

King Rehoboam's reign saw widespread homosexuality.

Abijah's stint was rift with civil war.

Self-appointed Zimri lasted seven days before he died on a regal pyre, having torched the palace to escape assassination.

Ahab and his First Lady, Jezebel, brought idol worship to new heights.

And Manasseh, whose name is synonymous with evil, practiced black magic, and fortunetelling. He even sacrificed his own son on a heathen altar.

Finally, the moral decadence of the Israelite leaders rendered the nation physically and spiritually impotent. For five centuries, God had honored their wishes, allowing Israel king after king. Now they were at the end of the trail. And they found it led them back to where they had begun—as captives in a faraway land.

## The Long-Awaited King

Sometimes, God waits a long time to make good on our mistakes. It was nearly four hundred years before He allowed another king on the scene. Then one starry night, God proclaimed a new king. A special coronation was held in Bethlehem. The palace was a stable, the throne a manger. And the infant ruler was in stark contrast with his predecessors.

This king was pure and gentle, humble and holy. This king was peace-loving, not warlike; wise, not foolish. This king is Jesus—the antithesis of that millennium between Saul and Himself. And though many Jews still do not recognize Him, He is the king for whom Israel was longing.

## Free to Decide

What would have happened if God had said "no" to this king business and sent Israel to bed without any supper? Could they have avoided centuries of idolatry? Perhaps. Might they have have missed out on Babylonian bondage? It's possible. But what does the typical eighth-grader do when his parent says, "No go"? He heads straight for the nearest puddle of trouble and dives in. He does precisely what his parent told him not to do, and with an extra pinch of rebelliousness. We can't be sure, but Israel probably would have done the same. But God gave them the freedom to decide, even though their decision was a bad one.

Are members of your family free to decide? Or is goal tending the predominant theme? If you answer, "yes" to the latter, I encourage you to gain a lesson from God: Learn to make the best of each other's bad decisions.

Obviously some discretion is necessary in this. Sometimes a parent must say "no" for the sake of the child's well-being. But as the child grows, he or she should be allowed to take more and more responsibility for decisions. And by all means, do not major in the minors—don't allow your rules to have more importance than your relationship with your children. This only provokes them to anger and bitterness. The child who is forced to leave the house with his shirttail in, will have it out by the time he rounds the corner.

Teens whose parents give them not only values but also the freedom to decide, usually do not stray from those values. They may rebel, but unlike the child who has been harnessed to the household rules, they don't resent their parents. Later they will feel free to return to the values that were important to their parents.

Finally, a spouse should never treat a spouse as a child. You are joined together in marriage to help one another reach your goals...not to slap them down. The marriage that is characterized by a consistent rejection of each others' ideas begins to resemble a parent-child relationship instead of the friend-friend covenant that marriage should be. Too many family fights are needlessly negative because of words like these:

"That's the most hideous hairdo I've ever seen. You head right back to the salon and have it fixed."

"Now dear, you're too old to start your own business. Besides, you're not trained for it."

Maybe the hairdo and the business venture *are* bad decisions. So was Israel's election of a king. But hair grows. The business might fly.

It took many crummy kings in order for God's children to learn a lesson. But God gave them the freedom to experience the worst. Then He gave them Christ, the picture of a true king. And in doing so, He made the best of their bad decisions.

# 28

# Anywhere But Here

When conflict makes the
door look inviting,
remember…

When angry barbs make
you want to back out,
remember…

He was falsely accused,
then sentenced to die—
but said nothing.

He stood still as they
covered him with spit.

When you come home
tired, and the conflict
awaiting you there is more
than you can handle,
remember…

When tongue-lashings
tempt you to flee,
remember…

When your castle seems a
circus, and you want to ab-
dicate the throne,
remember…

When you think, *Anywhere
but here would be nice*,
remember…

He was beaten, and
endured the blows.

He received in silence the
thirty-nine lashings from
the whip.

He was crowned with a
ring of thorns, and
kept on going.

Jesus longed for heaven,
but stayed…and prayed,
"Thy will be done."

# 29

# Breakfast by the Sea

"Checkmate!"
"Uncle!"
"Truce!"
A white flag waving.
Three slaps on the mat.
A mushroom cloud over Hiroshima.
Pulling out of 'Nam.
A divorce.

A breakfast by the sea.


There are dozens of ways to end a fight. But really…
*a breakfast by the sea?*
Yes! And it worked.
Have you ever offended someone, and then longed to
win back their friendship? That period between the rift
and the reunion is a desperate time. Waiting. Wondering. "Does she still love me?" "Does he still want me
around?" You know the feeling. And Peter, that impul-
sive, loud-mouthed disciple of Jesus, did too.
If words could kill, then Peter committed suicide a
thousand times. His tongue was his downfall, and on

one occasion he found himself at war with the Son of God.  Caught in the throes of an angry mob, Jesus was led away to be tried and sentenced for His claims of deity.  All but one of his friends deserted him.  Peter followed at a safe distance.  The mob marched on, through the courtyard gates and into the gaping jaws of the Praetorian Guard.  The doors slammed.  Peter hid in the shadows and wondered, "What will I say if I'm discovered?"  Soon he knew.

*"I don't even know him!"*  Peter spoke these five short words three separate times.  Jesus had predicted them.  Peter swore he would never say them.  Yet when recognized and questioned by a peasant woman, Peter denounced his affiliation with the Son of God.  Faced with a decision between death and freedom, Peter chose the latter.  Afterwards, he would have traded all the liberty in the world to be considered guilty by association with his Lord.  Less than a day later, Jesus was dead on a cross, and guilt tore through Peter like a Roman spike.

What offense is greater than denying a friend in the face of death?  If ever Jesus had the right to be upset, it was then.  When a best friend turns yellow just when he is most needed, then holding a grudge is perfectly justified—isn't it?  It's possible that Peter expected just that from Jesus—a God-sized grudge in return for his gossamer fidelity.

Three days later, Peter heard the news.  It was delivered by the women who went to anoint Jesus, but found an empty tomb instead.  An angel greeted them with these words:

> "Go, tell His disciples *and Peter*, 'He is going before you into Galilee; there you will see Him, just as He said to you.' "

I think that message was meant mostly for Peter. Note how he is singled out from the rest of the disciples. I can imagine Jesus dictating to that angel and making him repeat himself until he had it down just right, and especially the part about Peter. "Make <u>sure</u> that Peter knows I'm alive," was the point Jesus wanted the angel not to miss.

I wonder how Peter felt when he heard the news. Elated? Maybe. Relieved? Perhaps. But I think he also felt a little like the outlaw who ambushes Clint Eastwood and doesn't quite finish the job—"Nervous" with a capital N! It's terrible not knowing where you stand with someone you've offended.

"What will He think of me now?" Peter probably asked himself as he prepared his fishing nets to return to the work he had known all his life. His three years with Jesus seemed only a dream to him now, a blurred glimpse into the world of miracles and prophecies and spirits. Now he was back where he belonged—on the sea, with the familiar smells of wood, rope, salt, and fish. Here he could deal with the tangible and forget about the supernatural. Here he could mend nets and sails, and forget about mending blind men and beggars. Here he could fish for fish, and forget about fishing for men's souls.

But even if he set out to catch every fish in Galilee, he could not forget about Jesus before the task was done. He would not forget.

## *Pass the Fish*

One morning, after fishing all night with his friends and catching nothing, Peter spotted a thin line of smoke rising from the beach nearby. A man stooped over his fire and tended the breakfast that sizzled over it. The aroma drifted over the waves until it reached the boat full of hungry men, enticing them toward the shore.

"Any fish, boys?" the man shouted.

It was a familiar voice. Peter had heard it before. They all had. "No," replied the men. "We've caught nothing."

"Then throw your net on the right side and you'll get plenty of them," said the man.

With reluctance, the veteran fishermen obeyed the voice from the shore, for it sounded like a command—but without the arrogance. And they had nothing to lose.

Soon they hauled so many fish into the boat that there was barely room for the men. By now, everyone knew exactly who the man on the beach was. It was the Lord!

While they were still far off, Peter, in his excitement, leaped into the sea and swam toward the beach. As he swam he must have been thinking, "What will I say to him? What will I do?" Intellectually, Peter knew that he was forgiven. After all, the Jesus he had lived with for three years was in the habit of forgiving people who were much worse than he. But emotionally, Peter still felt cut off from the Lord. By the time he reached land he knew what he would do. He would busy himself with the catch of the day. And he did just that.

Picture Peter as he tried to avoid his friend, Jesus, whom he had denied just a short time before. Head down, hands moving fast, over-dramatizing his involvement with some knot, Peter was too busy to make eye contact, single-handedly hauling in the fish—one hundred and fifty-three large ones, to be exact—while his friends ate breakfast with Jesus.

Finally the job is done and Peter has nothing with which to occupy himself. His hands fidget, so he wipes them on his thighs. The men are quiet now; most of them are knee-deep in the sea, rinsing the grime of their trade from their tired bodies. The fire crackles behind him with a few fish waiting to be eaten. Jesus speaks.

"Peter. There's fish and bread here for you. Do you want them?"

Peter's eyes fill with tears. His face is still turned toward the sea, his back toward the fire. He is remembering mealtimes with Jesus. There was the wedding feast at Cana when Peter had first joined Jesus and His followers. When Jesus turned the water into wine and saved the groom from embarrassment, Peter knew he was following someone special.

He remembered the supper on the northern slopes of the Galilean sea, just east of Capernaum. That was a marvelous meal. Jesus praying over a handful of food and then feeding five thousand people with it. What a miracle! Finally, there was that last supper, the one he did not want to remember. At that meal, Jesus had spoken of betrayal and denial and death.

The tears begin to flow down Peter's face and collect in his beard. Then he feels a hand on his shoulder, and he hears the words he has longed to hear:

"Come, Peter. Your breakfast is almost cold. And by the way: I forgive you."

You would think that Jesus would say something like, "By the power invested in me, I hereby declare Peter guiltless and forgiven." But He didn't. Instead, He went beyond mere words. And with an ordinary token of service...a few morsels of food...He restored the big fisherman to his Lord.

The same simple types of service can help your family bring a fight to an end. Nothing else will do the trick. Not even "I'm sorry" or "I forgive you." For just as remorse must always be coupled with restitution, likewise remission must be linked with ritual.

When is the last time you ended a fight with someone in your family by *serving them?* Perhaps you feel that your efforts would prove unsuccessful if you tried. Or maybe you believe that you are above that sort of behavior. If that's the case, then remember Christ's example.

There was once a lonely fisherman, his life a shambles, his faith a wreck. So God gathered wood, squatted on a beach, lit a fire, and cooked him breakfast by the sea.

Checkmate!

Pass the fish!

# 30

# Mixed Nuts

I WOULD LIKE to register a complaint: *Buying Christmas presents is hard enough without being assaulted by shopping mall interviewers!*

You've seen these seemingly harmless people. They stand in the center of the mall with their clipboard and their questionnaire, waiting for some fool like me to make eye contact with them.

"Hi!" says the person sincerely. "Would you mind if I asked you a few hundred multiple-choice questions on a subject you probably know very little about?"

"Sure,"I say, despite the fact that I have my entire extended family to shop for. So the interview begins.

I recently wasted a valuable hour of gift-hunting because I was tricked into being queried on the topic of nuts, a jar of which I was promised for my cooperation. I assumed that I would be responding to a *few* simple questions concerning my nut preference, such as "Do you like nuts?" and, "If so, what kind?" One glance at the survey told me my assumption was a grave oversight.

My interrogator led me and my infant son up a long flights of stairs. At the top we turned left and proceeded down a dark corridor which looked like the backstage of a theater. We were in the bowels of the mall. Naked wires hung like entrails from the ceiling, and insulation peered from behind broken drywall. "Here we are," the woman said as she opened the door to a tiny, smoke-filled room, invited me in, and ordered me to take a seat. I knew she believed in miracles when she said, "Make yourself comfortable."

I perched stiffly on the cold, folding chair, clutching my son to my chest and feeling guilty for dragging him into this. After all, he thought we were coming to the mall for a picture with Santa.

Ten minutes passed. Then twenty. Then thirty. Still the questions kept coming.

"Which is more important to you—the freshness of a nut, or its roasted flavor?"

"What size nut is most appealing to you?"

"How many times would you say you have eaten nuts in the last five years? Please be specific."

Finally, after an hour, the ordeal ended. My son was making it known that he wanted to leave.

When I asked the woman if I could go, she said, "Wait a minute. Aren't you forgetting one thing?"

I froze. I could feel my forehead tightening and I thought, "If she asks me one more question, I'm going to scream."

She continued: "Your free can of nuts, sir. You do want them, don't you?"

I breathed easy. Free nuts? Of course I wanted them. I'll hardly ever turn down a nut, because I enjoy almost every kind except...

"Mixed nuts!" she said, pulling the jar from a brown paper bag.

Aaaghhh! My worst nightmare. After an hour of painful inquisition, I was being compensated for my efforts with the only food in the world that rivals a Christmas fruitcake...mixed nuts!

I have always believed nuts were meant to be segregated. Nothing is worse than putting a good nut in the same can with a bad nut. And the definition of a bad nut can be summed up in one word: *filbert.* I don't know the filbert's origin, but this nut has ruined more than one New Year's Eve for me by sneaking into my mouth undetected. It's to these pesky, little intruders that I attribute my disdain for mixed nuts.

## *The Nutty Disciples*

Jesus Christ championed the cause of mixed nuts during His earthly ministry. If ever there was variety in one can, it was found in His own little band of men, handpicked by the Master to be His closest companions. Four of the Twelve were fishermen, one a tax collector, and another a member of an extremist guerrilla group. Quite a blend, don't you agree?

I have often wondered why Jesus chose men from such contrasting walks of life. Surely He expected trouble. He could not have overlooked the fact that a Jewish tax collector working for the Roman government might at least slightly irritate a zealot who was diametrically opposed to Rome's involvement in Judea, not to mention the fact that both tax collector and zealot would pose a threat to the simple fishermen, whose only cause in life was to catch fish.

If Jesus knew these facts ahead of time, why did He choose the men He did? Could He not have searched throughout Israel and found twelve men more suitable— and compatible—for the job of spreading the gospel? If so, why didn't He? The answer is simple.

Jesus likes mixed nuts!

And He has used them throughout history to feed a world starving for truth and life. Do you see the beauty of His plan? Jesus uses walnuts, and peanuts, and pecans, and cashews, and yes, even filberts, to get the job done.  And His desire is that they *all* live in harmony.

Jesus was once asked by His disciples to decide an argument between them about who was the greatest.  In essence, Jesus told them, "You nuts!  None of you is greater than the other.  You are all part of the same can, and you only become great by serving one another."

The same is true of your marriage and your family.

*mixed nuts*

Inevitably, your household will be a vaudeville of assorted nuts.

## *The Family Filbert*

Is there a filbert in your family? Do you look upon him with disgust because he is different from you? Do you ever find yourself conflicting with the family filbert because the two of you do not think alike, or dress alike, or talk alike, or do anything alike? If so, then you need to ask yourself *Why?*

"Why do I get so bent when others do not conform to my plans or my wishes?"

"Why do I feel so frustrated when someone else does not share my values?"

Why do I expect my spouse to always think like me?"

Perhaps, like me, you are prejudiced against filberts and would prefer that your family be filled exclusively with nuts of your own kind. I know the feeling. On too many occasions I have demanded that Cindy think, act, and feel exactly like me. If you haven't learned *your* lesson yet, take a closer look at Jesus' ragtag bunch of nutty disciples. Despite their diversity, their unity astounded the world and gave appeal to the message of Christ.

The men that Jesus chose to be His disciples had no special qualifications. They were not rich, nor did they hold high positions in society. They were not trained pastors or teachers or church officials. They were twelve ordinary men selected by Jesus to live together as an example of Christian love. Sure, they had conflicts. But at the core of their relationships was the acceptance of one another's uniqueness. No one expected the walnut to be a cashew, or the pecan to think like the peanut. All that mattered was that each one submitted to Jesus.

Are you willing to live in a mixed can? Your ability to conflict with one another depends on it. God has purposely designed each member of your little can to be different. For instance, big daddy walnut may be extremely athletic, but his son, the peanut, may have a flair for the intellectual. Can the two of them come together to form a nice, roasted blend? Yes. It's possible. But some families refuse to reach for this level of tolerance. Therefore, they can never learn to enjoy a family fight. When engaged in conflict, the conservative cashew, who has no patience with the prodigal pecan, will probably break all the rules in the book, and the pecan will do likewise.

All over the world are millions of mixed cans. And regardless of whether they live in mansions or slums, all are faced with the same problem of acceptance.

How about your can? Have you embraced one another's individual nuttiness? Perhaps you have tried, but still do not know how. Why not look to Jesus? He has already shown the way. And it is He who is the Lord of the can.

# 31

# Keeper of the Greens

DAVID SPENT A SUMMER watching the grass grow. He had nursed her from bare clod to brilliant carpet. And with the coming of autumn, he mourned the loss of a child.

I cannot understand my friend's grief; but, unlike David, I am not a golf course groundskeeper. I have never been the midwife to Mother Terra as she brought forth lawn, nor have I guarded her tender offspring through fiery July. Nor have I known the pain of watching my adopted babies be trampled by spike-clad businessmen and bombarded by golf balls. This is why I show little emotion at the autumn death of a golf course.

I suppose that only one who has tilled the soil, sown the seed, watered the turf, and mown the blade can truly feel as David does year after year. God in heaven knows the feeling.

From dust, God created man. And out of man, He fashioned woman. As their Keeper, His design was for them to flourish and to become lush and green. And He provided the perfect climate for them to do so. They were to God as the green is to the groundskeeper—precious and beautiful.

But something spoiled God's greens. It was sin. And

in sorrow, He watched their color fade from bright emer-
ald to pasty grey. Yet, He did not abandon them. Even
today, He kneels faithfully and fixes the divots with a
tool called forgiveness. No divot is too big for Him to repair.

Rummage through the pages of the New Testament
and you will uncover some pathetic men and women
whose lives were divoted by sin. One in particular
stands out in the eighth chapter of John's gospel.

## *The Divot Called Adultery*

Half-naked and dirty, the woman was dragged to
Jesus and thrown at His feet.

"Take a look at her!" shouted her accusers, the religious leaders of Jerusalem. "We caught her red-handed.
What should her punishment be?"

Clearly the woman was at fault. She had committed
one of the three gravest sins of her day—adultery, which,
along with murder and idolatry, was punishable by
death...by stoning. The smug Pharisees stood with their
arms folded, waiting for Jesus' answer. If He condemned
her, He would be stripped of the title "Friend of sinners,"
and would lose His following. If He set her free, they
could accuse Him of teaching others to defy Jewish law.
They had Him cornered, or so they thought.

Jesus surprised them all. He had compassion for the
woman. He saw her in a manner unlike the Pharisees
did. True, she was in conflict with God. She had willful-
ly broken one of His commandments. By choice she had
put a monumental divot in her life. And she had severely damaged one of God's greens. Had she not been con-
fronted by the Pharisees, she would probably have gone
on sinning, leaving behind her a trail of unfixed divots.
But Jesus envisioned her as she was meant to b-

be—smooth, and soft, and perfect. Instead of naked and ashamed, He saw her clothed and full of integrity. Rather than empty and searching, He saw her brimming with joy.

To the Pharisees He said, "Okay. Go right ahead and stone her. But let him whose life is void of divots cast the first stone."

Slowly, the crowd dispersed. Soon the woman was left standing alone with Jesus.

"Where are your accusers?" said Jesus. "Didn't even one of them condemn you?"

"No, sir," she said.

"Neither do I," Jesus said. "Go and sin no more."

The woman came to Jesus with a sin-pocked life, and walked away forgiven. She had met the Keeper of the Greens... and He had fixed her divots.

## *Thou Shalt Not...*

Cindy and I love to take walks, and one of our favorite places to do so is on a golf course, late at night. Far from street lights and blaring horns, we stroll down fairways arm in arm. Here, water and sand bedeck the ground like jewels in the moonlight. The greens are groomed perfectly for the morning. Everything is serene. It is our escape from the clamor of the city.

I have often wished that all of life could be flawless and tranquil. The Pharisees wanted the same. They longed for a world where everything was in order and the rules were kept. But they were unwilling to deal with divots. Are you?

Take a divot inventory of your household. Start by checking your own list of do's and don'ts. Every family member has one of these, whether it is written on paper or kept in the head. It is their "Ten Commandments for

How a Family Should Be Run". I'll bet you have one, too. Here are a few entries from the list Cindy and I keep:

> Thou shalt not make entries into the checkbook without subtracting.
> Thou shalt not wear muddy shoes in the house.
> Thou shalt not leave home with the curling iron turned on.
> Thou shalt not gamble on a low gas tank.
> Thou shalt not leave the toilet paper roll empty.

Perhaps you recognize one or two of these. Undoubtedly, you have some of your own. And you can be sure that each time one of your commandments is broken, another divot is driven into your life. Often, the offender neglects repairing the damage. He or she wanders off without so much as a simple "I'm sorry". That's usually when the sparks begin to fly.

Most family fights start when one member sins against another. Is there any rule on your list so sacred that, if it was violated, you would stone a loved one with angry words—or reject him altogether? I hope not.

Successful family fights depend on forgiveness. That doesn't mean that you must abandon your "Ten Commandments" list and let others walk all over you. Jesus did not do that. To the woman caught in adultery, He said, "Go and sin no more." Nevertheless, Jesus was tender and compassionate. You and I must be, also.

## Family Forgiveness

Imagine your family as a group of people walking down the fairway of life together. I assume that each person in your group is taking his or her best shot at this crazy game called "family living."

In the quest for the cup (a family's attempt to get along with one another), some divots will be created, and certain team members will be angry or hurt. That's when forgiveness is needed. But unlike fixing divots in golf, forgiveness requires a lot more of you than merely bending down to do a little smoothing. Sometimes it requires you to fix a divot that someone else has caused. And that takes a lot of patience and understanding.

Like my friend David, you will forever be searching for a balance between demanding perfection and learning to live with imperfection. Some of your worst fights will occur when you expect the former and are intolerant of the latter. If he could have it his way, David would have preferred that no golfers ever came to the course. That way his greens would always be an inerrant reflection of his handiwork. Instead, his job required him to put up with divots. Many evenings, David felt embittered by the insensitivities of those who seemed to hold little respect for his work. As they loaded their clubs in their car trunks and headed for home, they didn't realize the time it would cost him to resurrect their playground for the following day.

Embittered. Isn't that how you feel at times? Just when things in the family are running smoothly, (which usually means they are going *your* way), a new day begins and some family member assaults your "green." They will "tee off" on your idea of what life should be like. They will break your commandments. When this happens, you are faced with some options. You can either whack some heads with your nine iron, or you can choose to become a "divot fixer." What will you do?

# 32

# Scarlet Emotion

WHENEVER I AM TEMPTED to tell a lie, I remember two things: my eighth-grade "tonsillectomy" and the pathetic figure of Reverend Dimmesdale.

I was thirteen and in love with Donna, the goddess of Hoover Junior High. She was the only reason to stay awake in English class, where we were being introduced to Hawthorne's *The Scarlet Letter*, the story of the adulterous secret between Hester Prynne and her beloved pastor, Arthur Dimmesdale. Though Hester's sin was uncovered, the reverend's was not. And the congregation was fooled by his pseudo-saintliness. This is the classic tale of a man trapped in a lie.

Because both our last names began with "C" I sat directly behind Donna. But as far as she was concerned, our relationship was purely alphabetical. She was in love with a boy named Andy, who ignored her affection for a very good reason. Andy hated girls.

Day after day, I studied Donna's hair and the way she held her pencil, and how she looked whenever she was trying to remember an answer on a test. And then I would look across the room at Andy and ask myself, "What does he have that I don't?" And then, one day it came to me: *Andy had a broken leg.*

I had discovered the key to a girl's heart, and it was this: "Girls are attracted to wounded boys!" I had found a way to win Donna's love. Now all I needed to do was injure myself. I ran down a mental list of impairments, searching for the best sympathy inducer. Broken arm? Too painful. Head cold? Too common. Black Plague? Too conspicuous. Tonsillectomy? Perfect!

That Friday afternoon, I announced to Donna my pending surgery. And I rode the bus home enraptured with the memory of her response. How conveniently I had misinterpreted her question of "Will it hurt?" to mean so much more. But it wasn't until I began considering the logistics of a tonsillectomy that I realized I had a serious problem.

I had a throatful of perfectly healthy tonsils, with no surgery in the forecast. Monday morning was looming like the gallows. And like the Reverend Dimmesdale, I was frantic. Would I be discovered? Would my story be made known to the entire school?

I devised a plan. If I could not have my tonsils out, I could at least "do them in". Out to the back yard I went, checking first to make certain no one was listening. I was alone.

Standing in freezing temperatures, wearing only a T-shirt, I screamed for a solid hour. And when I finished, I sounded as if I'd had not only my tonsils removed, but my entire throat as well. Now I could only wait.

Monday morning came, and the teacher asked me to read aloud. My heart raced. At any moment I felt as if my own scarlet letter would burn its way through my chest, leaving a bright red "L" for all to see, branding me as a liar. I stood and opened my book to the place where we had ended the week prior. Here before me was Dimmesdale's confession. And it seemed as if the printed page itself was my own admission of guilt. My voice cracked and rasped as I read.

"Now, at the death-hour, he stands up before you! He bids you look again at Hester's scarlet letter! He tells you, that, with all its mysterious horror, it is but the shadow of what he bears on his own breast, and that even this, his own red stigma, is no more than the type of what has seared his inmost heart!"

I finished and sat down. Not a soul was aware of my trickery. I basked in the glory of sympathetic smiles.

The plan had worked though not to the extent that Donna ever became my girlfriend. In fact, to her I was never anything more than just another "C" in the same row. However, I was spared the embarrassment of being caught in a lie. And in the process, I learned a valuable lesson.

> *When dishonesty of any kind is held inside, it burns one's soul like a scarlet letter.*

## Heartburn

We should all learn a lesson from the good Reverend Dimmesdale, and from our own experiences with dark, inner secrets—those devilish thoughts and feelings and memories that were never meant to be imprisoned in our souls. One such feeling is anger. It can burn a hole through the very walls of one's heart. Thousands around the world are seared with its flaming "A". It is the scarlet emotion. And unlike my fortunate escape from the consequences of my lie to Donna, you can never elude its grasp. Are you one of those who suffer from heartburn? If so, then the following scripture is recommended medicine. To the Ephesians, Paul said,

> *Be angry*, yet do not sin. Don't let the sun go down on your anger.

This is a strange command. Haven't you been told all your life that anger is to be avoided? Didn't Christ say that, "If you are angry, even in your own home, you are in danger of judgment"? But Paul, in his plea to Ephesus for proper Christian relationships, is telling us to embrace the very thing we shun. It doesn't make sense! Or does it? Here are three considerations.

## Consider...

Two Greek words in the New Testament are used to denote anger. One is *thumos*, the other is *orge*. *Thumos* is that fire which flares up quickly, but just as easily dies down. We all have seen a pile of autumn leaves burning in late October, and have wished that the aroma could linger forever. But all too soon, the flame ceases and the sweet smoke drifts to other neighborhoods. *Thumos* anger is like that.

On the other hand, *orge* is a slow-burning fire, like the blaze of a tar pit smoldering at leisure. There is no pleasant fragrance here. And the stench seems endless. *Orge* anger is like that. This is the anger Christ wants us to avoid.

The person who expresses his anger in a *thumos* way gets it over with quickly. He or she keeps short accounts of anger. But the person who uses *orge* anger keeps it always inside...on "slow burn". This is the person who has an eye for revenge. We have all known people like this, and they are usually bitter or depressed.

All fire is potentially dangerous, but that doesn't stop us from using it for the good of humanity. Prehistoric man deemed fire a gift from the gods, and he neither ran from it nor abused it. Instead he respected it. Likewise, all anger is potentially dangerous. Therefore, we must decide how we will use it. What decision have you made about handling anger? Are you a sweet pile of crackling leaves? Or a dark, stifling tar pit?

## Consider...

If you reverse the order of the phrases in Ephesians 4:26, you end up with something like this: *"Don't* be angry, and wind up sinning."

And who do you suppose is the primary victim of your sin? That's right! *You.* Like Reverend Dimmesdale, you will find that the pain of your own scarlet "A" burns hotter with every moment you keep it inside.

## Consider...

Paul preceded verse 26 in Ephesians 4 with this command:

> Stop lying to each other; tell the truth, for we are parts of each other and when we lie to each other we are hurting *ourselves.*

Suppressed anger is a wicked lie, indeed! It is the unsurpassed example of "false advertisement." It is the burning bosom masked by a saintly smile. And yet, on and on it smolders, lingering always between depression and rage. But God never intended us to live this way.

## Honestly Angry

If this chapter describes you, I want to leave you with these simple thoughts. You can do two things to rid yourself of that bloody "A". First, you can tell the truth. If you're mad, admit it. Don't say everything is fine when your heart is burning like hell.

Finally, when you have taken the first step toward emotional honesty, commit yourself to following the rules outlined in this book. They will help to keep you from returning to your old deceitful ways. They will make your family fights more enjoyable. And they will give you some guidelines within which you can express your anger constructively.

My prayer is that God will bless you in your attempts to become honestly angry, and that He will replace your scarlet emotion with a peace that is whiter than snow.

# 33

# The Tax Man Who Got Hooked

ANYONE SERIOUS about becoming a skillful fisherman must have a mentor. And I can tell you how to find one.

First, ignore the folks with the fancy equipment. Fast boats and bass-finders are impressive, but their owner's fish knowledge does not always match his pocketbook. Instead, seek diligently for the unexpected.

The crusty codger with the three-day stubble is the type to look for. You can find him on the banks of most any lake, planted firmly in a patio chair.

Everything he does goes against the book. Rather than fish by the inlet, or the outlet, or a mossy point, he stakes his claim at some unlikely spot and there he spends the entire day. And he always seems to catch fish.

He is the man who has, at most, three lures in his tackle box—each of them his favorite. He may not look like much, but he can tell you when the fish are spawning, and what they're biting on. He can also instruct you in the proper way to clean a fish. And if you're lucky, he might even share a family recipe or two with you. Once you have found your mentor, sit at his feet for a while and learn all you can. Your time will not be wasted.

You'll also need a mentor if you want to become a proficient family fighter. I can think of no one better to teach you the trade than Jesus of Nazareth. On the subject of family fighting, He certainly is the unexpected mentor. After all, the Bible indicates that He never even dated, let alone take a wife or father a child. Yet, He resolved conflicts with men and women as effortlessly as the veteran angler lands his limit.

As I suggested earlier, most of us spend our lives complaining about "the one that got away." But the truth is that our loved ones don't get away—we frighten them away. It's no wonder we're starved for intimacy.

Let's look at how the principle of "matching the hatch"—of wooing and winning those with whom we may be in conflict—was put into action by the most famous fisherman of all time, Jesus Christ.

## Fishing in Jericho

It was morning, and Jesus was going fishing. His disciples gathered around Him.

"Where are we traveling today, good Master?" they asked Him. "Shall we try our luck in the Sea of Galilee?"

"We're going to Jericho," He replied, "to fish for men."

Awaiting them in Jericho were crowded streets heaving with the ebb and flow of human life, a flood in which the elite and the common folk moved side by side. Into this bay of souls, Jesus cast His nets.

"Jesus is coming! Jesus is coming! Hurry! He is about to begin his teaching."

The masses had heard of this teacher from Nazareth. Travelers making the trek between Jerusalem and Capernaum brought news of his ministry. The sick and lame were especially curious to see Jesus, for there were reports that he could heal. As Jesus walked along the dusty thoroughfare, the crowds became more dense in his wake.

From a distance, a man watched jealously. He was a small Jewish man, hated by every citizen of Jericho, a renegade tax man who filled Caesar's purse with his brothers' wages. Though he had immense wealth, he was like a man plagued with scurvy, lacking the one thing he needed most. His name was Zacchaeus and he needed a friend.

Soon the crowd engulfed Zacchaeus, and he was caught in the undertow. To escape, he climbed a sycamore tree. He wedged himself between two thick branches and watched.

*There,* he thought. *Now I can have a look at Him.*

He was strangely attracted to Jesus. Something about this respected religious teacher—a man who socialized with beggars and prostitutes—gave hope to Zacchaeus's lonely heart. Perhaps here was the key to happiness. He had tried everything else, and had paid a high price along the way. Now he was alone—alone with his money, alone with his thoughts, alone in a tree.

"Hello up there!"

Suddenly Zacchaeus was startled back into the present. He looked down to see Jesus smiling up at him. Laughter filled the streets below. Fingers pointed. Heads wagged.

"Look at the little man...like a cat in a tree!"

"Careful, Zacchaeus. You might spoil your fine clothes."

Jesus spoke again. "Zacchaeus, you are just the man I have been looking for. I would be honored to be a guest in your house today. Quick! Come down and join me."

No doubt Zacchaeus nearly fell out of his leafy perch that day. And I'll wager the crowd wasn't laughing anymore. They were probably shocked at Jesus' choice of hosts, and must have murmured to themselves, "Does He know what He's doing? Does He know who He's talking to?"

Jesus knew exactly what He was doing and to whom He was speaking. He was matching the hatch with the most despised man in Jericho. For bait He used love, something Zacchaeus hadn't tasted in years. And the result was another lost person reeled into the Kingdom of God.

Listen to what the changed Zacchaeus said to Jesus:

"Sir, from now on I will give half my wealth to the poor, and if I find I have overcharged anyone on his taxes, I will penalize myself by giving him back four times as much!"

That's radical transformation!

## *The Choicest Lure*

Take a closer look now at the facts. As the Bible indicates, here is Jesus journeying from Galilee to Judea to be impaled on a cross. En route, He stops in Jericho, where he encounters an employee of the very government that will enforce His capital punishment. Zacchaeus was in conflict with Jesus, for he served money rather than God. To our surprise, Jesus responds with love. No sermons on mammon worship. No bitter chastening. Merely a loving word of respect. Instantly, Zacchaeus is changed.

How many times have you been in conflict with your spouse over a difference of opinion? The more you tried to change his or her perspective, the wider the chasm grew between you. In your attempts to reel them in toward your way of thinking, you lost them altogether.

Rather than "matching the hatch," you threw out the wrong bait.

Jesus wants to be your mentor. In His possession are three of His favorite lures—

faith...

hope...

and love.

To the skeptic and the downtrodden, He casts the first two. But for the Zacchaeuses of the world, He knows that only the third will do.

Is there a Zacchaeus in your household—someone who, in your opinion, takes advantage of you and the rest of the family? If so, I challenge you to approach that person in a different manner. The next time the two of you are in conflict, stop for a moment and consider the ways of the world's greatest fisherman. Then dig deep into your tackle box and offer your opponent the choicest of lures.

# 34

# Bridge

EVERY FALL, Cindy and I return to Branson. We go to visit old friends, and to walk in the woods. We go to experience the Ozark Mountain Crafts Festival, and to eat at Uncle Joe's Barbecue, and to jog on Cougar Trail. We go for the cider, and the geese, and the kaleidoscope leaves.

But most of all we go to remember.

This past fall we took our new little boy, Wesley—Wesley Klein Cunningham. The "Klein" is in honor of the volunteer fireman who pulled us from the wreckage on Bee Creek Bridge that cold December morning.

On our last day in town, we telephoned Klein to let him know about our son. He was proud. "I never had anybody take my name before," he said.

"We've made a lot of changes on that bridge since you two had your wreck" Klein told us. "That was a mighty slick patch of highway before we got to it. But we haven't had trouble since we put that new surface down. People go whizzing through all year long like they were on an L.A. freeway.

"And another thing," he continued: "We had to make a special tool right there on the spot to pry your little Cindy out. We ended up getting a patent on the thing. Now it's helping folks all over the country."

Then Cindy got on the phone and she and Klein chatted about the color of Wesley's hair, and how much he weighed, and whether or not we spelled 'Klein' the same way he did. Then we said goodbye and headed for home.

We drove north out of town, past the Dairy Queen, and Skaggs Memorial Hospital, and Branson High School—home of the fighting Pirates.

Soon the bridge was in sight, and Cindy squeezed my hand.

As we drove onto the iron trestle, the wheels of our Honda whined as they gripped the grooves carved into the surface for safety. We were thankful for the change. But one thing was not changed: There on the east guard rail were the distinct markings of our wintry wreck, markings still untouched after seven years—a copper-toned testimony of the gift of pain.

I thought about all the people who had benefitted from our pain. Klein had given his life to Christ at the scene of the accident. Later, his wife and daughter did the same. Then there are those thousands of travelers who safely cross that bridge each year unaware of the improvements that were made as a result of our accident. Finally, I thought of Cindy and myself. We received the greatest blessing—each other. And we have a son who is a daily reminder of the lighter side of pain.

I thought also of all the people like you who would one day read this book, many of them so afraid of conflict with one another that they have only two ways to handle it when it arises: attack or avoid. Consequently, they never venture onto the bridge, because it seems so foreboding. If only they could taste of the truly satisfying relationships that await them on the other side.

NOW YOU HAVE COME to the bottom of the gift box. No more rules. No more styles. You are alone amid the wrappings. Perhaps you believe now that conflict can be a positive experience for you and your family. If so, I encourage you to get to know the Master of conflict and hold fast to His rules.

On the other hand, you may still be a skeptic who can't possibly imagine how your family could benefit from a fight. If that's the case, I don't blame you. After all, icy roads and rattlesnakes are never nice. But then again...Bee Creek Bridge was an unlikely place to begin a romance.